Great Expect

CHARLES DICKENS

Oxford
Literature
Companions

Notes and activities: Su Fielder
Series consultant: Peter Buckroyd

OXFORD
UNIVERSITY PRESS

Contents

Language   70

Themes   84

Skills and Practice   98

Glossary   110

Introduction

What are Oxford Literature Companions?

Oxford Literature Companions is a series designed to provide you with comprehensive support for popular set texts. You can use the Companion alongside your novel, using relevant sections during your studies or using the book as a whole for revision.

Each Companion includes detailed guidance and practical activities on:

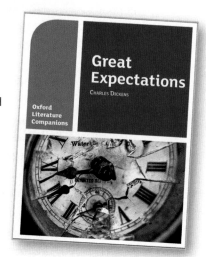

- **Plot and Structure**
- **Context**
- **Characters**
- **Language**
- **Themes**
- **Skills and Practice**

How does this book help with exam preparation?

As well as providing guidance on key areas of the novel, throughout this book you will also find 'Upgrade' features. These are tips to help with your exam preparation and performance.

In addition, in the extensive **Skills and Practice** chapter, the 'Preparing for your assessment' section provides detailed guidance on areas such as how to prepare for the exam, understanding the question, planning your response and hints for what to do (or not do) in the exam.

In the **Skills and Practice** chapter there is also a bank of **Sample questions** and **Sample answers**. The **Sample answers** are marked and include annotations and a summative comment.

How does this book help with terminology?

Throughout the book, key terms are **highlighted** in the text and explained on the same page. There is also a detailed **Glossary** at the end of the book that explains, in the context of the novel, all the relevant literary terms highlighted in this book.

Which edition of the novel has this book used?

Quotations have been taken from the Oxford University Press Rollercoaster edition of *Great Expectations* (ISBN: 9780198355342), which refers to Chapters 1-59 consecutively.

Other editions restart chapter numbering at the beginning of each volume. If using one of these editions, the chart below can be used to convert the chapter number references in this Oxford Literature Companion:

	Chapter numbers																			
Volume 1	1	2	3	4	5	6	7	8	9	10	11	12	13	14	15	16	17	18	19	
	1	2	3	4	5	6	7	8	9	10	11	12	13	14	15	16	17	18	19	
Volume 2	20	21	22	23	24	25	26	27	28	29	30	31	32	33	34	35	36	37	38	39
	1	2	3	4	5	6	7	8	9	10	11	12	13	14	15	16	17	18	19	20
Volume 3	40	41	42	43	44	45	46	47	48	49	50	51	52	53	54	55	56	57	58	59
	1	2	3	4	5	6	7	8	9	10	11	12	13	14	15	16	17	18	19	20

How does this book work?

Each book in the Oxford Literature Companions series follows the same approach and includes the following features:

- **Key quotations** from the novel
- **Key terms** explained on the page and linked to a complete glossary at the end of the book
- **Activity boxes** to help improve your understanding of the text
- **Upgrade** tips to help prepare you for your assessment

Plot

Volume 1, Chapters 1–3

The novel's narrator explains how, as a child, he came to be called Pip. He remembers one Christmas Eve when he was pounced on by a fierce convict, in a lonely churchyard, and threatened with violence unless he agreed to fetch the convict food and a file. The convict describes an accomplice who likes to get at the hearts and livers of small boys. Terrified, Pip agrees to help him and runs home to the forge where he lives with his elder sister and her husband, Joe Gargery, the blacksmith.

Angry with him for being late for his tea, Mrs Joe beats Pip with a cane nicknamed Tickler. Before he goes to bed, Pip hears the sound of a gunshot from the **Hulks**, signalling the escape of another convict. Pip gets up at dawn to rob the pantry and also takes a file from the forge for the convict.

Pip secretly sets out across the marshes, feeling very guilty about stealing from his sister. Pip watches 'his' convict greedily devour the smuggled food and drink, telling him that he is **"glad you enjoy it"** *(Volume 1, Chapter 3)* but warning that **"There's no more to be got where that came from"** *(Volume 1, Chapter 3)*, having seen the second convict that he took to be the dangerous **'young man'** *(Volume 1, Chapter 3)*. At this, 'his' convict desperately begins to file away the clasp of his leg-iron, telling Pip he will track the other convict **"down, like a bloodhound"** *(Volume 1, Chapter 3)*.

- Young Pip's story is narrated as if by an older and wiser Pip; his name reminds us of a seed that will grow into a healthy mature plant; names are significant in this story.

- Mrs Joe's violent treatment of the brother she boasts to have brought up **'by hand'** *(Volume 1, Chapter 2)* contrasts with Joe's attempt to protect Pip and introduces the theme of good and bad 'parenting'.

- Pip's compassion for the convict, despite his fierce looks, and the convict's gratitude to Pip in return, create an unspoken bond between them.

The convict terrifies young Pip
(*Great Expectations*, 2012)

> **Key quotations**
>
> A fearful man, all in coarse grey, with a great iron on his leg. A man with no hat, and with broken shoes, and with an old rag tied round his head. A man who had been soaked in water, and smothered in mud, and lamed by stones, and cut by flints, and stung by nettles, and torn by briars; who limped, and shivered, and glared, and growled... *(Volume 1, Chapter 1)*

> **Activity 1**
>
> Although Pip is terrified by the sight of the convict, Dickens presents a rather pitiable figure. How does Dickens achieve that effect in the quotation above? Think about Dickens's choice of words and sentence structure.

Volume 1, Chapters 4–6

Pip suffers terrible guilt and apprehension throughout the Christmas dinner attended by Mr Wopsle, the arrogant church clerk, Mr Hubble the wheelwright and his wife, and Uncle Pumblechook, a self-important **corn-chandler**. Their conversation revolves around Pip's 'ingratitude' to his sister's 'kindness' in bringing him up. Just before Mrs Joe discovers the theft of her pork pie, Pip runs from the table, to be stopped by a party of soldiers looking for the blacksmith to mend a pair of handcuffs.

> **corn-chandler** a trader who sells corn
>
> **Hulks** old warships moored in rivers and harbours served as temporary prisons at the time the novel was set, used when regular prisons were full to capacity

The soldiers are out searching for the escaped convicts and allow Joe, Pip and Mr Wopsle to join the hunt. The two convicts are discovered fighting in a ditch; Pip's convict (Magwitch) boasts about having prevented the other fellow's escape, telling the soldiers, **"He's a gentleman, if you please, this villain"** *(Volume 1, Chapter 5)*. Both are arrested and returned to the Hulks. Pip signals to his convict that he was not responsible for leading the soldiers to him. In return, Magwitch confesses to having stolen food from the blacksmith's house to protect Pip from blame.

Back at the forge, the grown-ups puzzle over how the convict could have broken in to steal the food. Although he wanted to tell Joe the truth, Pip was worried that this would lose him Joe's good opinion and trust.

- Pip's guilty conscience is a consistent theme throughout the novel.
- Dickens often gives 'silly' names to his exaggeratedly comical characters, making it impossible for the reader to take them seriously.
- The theme of what it is to be a gentleman is introduced here as Magwitch calls the second convict both a 'gentleman' and a 'villain'.

Activity 2

The description of the Christmas celebration reveals that, although Pip's sister was often harsh towards Pip, his childhood was spent in relative comfort. Go back through Chapter 3, looking for clues about the way the Gargery household lived.

Key quotations

By the light of the torches, we saw the black Hulk lying out a little way from the mud of the shore, like a wicked Noah's ark. *(Volume 1, Chapter 5)*

… I was too cowardly to do what I knew to be right, as I had been too cowardly to avoid doing what I knew to be wrong. *(Volume 1, Chapter 6)*

Key facts about Noah's ark

According to the Bible (Genesis, Chapters 6–8), Noah built his 'Ark' at God's request to save his family and every species of the animal kingdom from the great flood; this 'wicked' Noah's Ark 'protects' society from the wickedness contained within it. Magwitch and Compeyson are taken on board 'two by two' (like Noah's animals); the one a **'varmint'** *(Volume 1, Chapter 3)* and the other a 'gentleman', like two strains of the same species.

Volume 1, Chapters 7 and 8

Pip describes his early schooling in chaotic evening classes run by Mr Wopsle's great aunt. Joe explains how he missed out on school as he had to work to support his mother and his violent, alcoholic father. He recalls how gladly he welcomed Pip to the forge when Mrs Joe agreed to marry him and we understand why he tolerates her fiery temper. Joe's history affects little Pip who **'had a new sensation of feeling conscious that I was looking up to Joe in my heart'** *(Volume 1, Chapter 7)*.

Mrs Joe and Uncle Pumblechook announce that Pip is to go and 'play' at the request of Miss Havisham, **'an immensely rich and grim lady… who led a life of seclusion'** *(Volume 1, Chapter 7)*.

When Pip goes to Satis House the next day he sees **'the strangest lady I have ever seen, or shall ever see'** *(Volume 1, Chapter 8)*. Miss Havisham lives in suspended time with all clocks stopped at twenty to nine. Pip is too bewildered to 'play', at first. When Estella and Pip play cards together, Estella calls Pip a **"common labouring-boy"** with **"coarse hands"** and **"thick boots"** *(Volume 1, Chapter 8)*, insults he never forgets.

- Joe's Christian virtues of forgiveness (for his father, who he maintains was **"good in his hart"** *(Volume 1, Chapter 7)*, and charity (in taking in little Pip when he married his sister) are revealed.

- Dickens introduces the theme of the value of education as a tool for self-improvement.
- The notion that Miss Havisham might make Pip's fortune originates here, in the **avaricious** imaginations of Mrs Joe and Uncle Pumblechook.

avaricious greedy for money or personal gain

varmint (Magwitch pronounces it 'warmint') the local dialect version of 'vermin', the name given to troublesome small animals or insects such as rats and cockroaches

Key quotations

"... this boy's fortune may be made by his going to Miss Havisham's"
(Volume 1, Chapter 7)

Activity 3

In groups of three, (Pip, Joe and 'narrator') read aloud from **"Why didn't you ever go to school, Joe, when you were as little as me?"** to **"... but this is the up-and-down-and-straight on it, Pip, and I hope you'll overlook short-comings"** *(Volume 1, Chapter 7)*. Then, discuss:

a) what we learn about Joe's attitude towards his parents and towards his wife

b) how the older Pip's comments help us to visualize the scene.

Key facts about Victorian Dame schools

Dame schools, of the type run by Wopsle's great aunt, typically provided cheap, yet generally inadequate, schooling to poor children.

Volume 1, Chapters 9 and 10

Mrs Joe and Uncle Pumblechook quiz Pip about his visit to Miss Havisham's. Pip invents an elaborate lie about a game involving a black velvet coach, flags, swords, big dogs and veal cutlets. The adults are completely taken in and begin to speculate about what else Miss Havisham might do for Pip. Later, Pip confesses to Joe, who gives Pip a kindly warning against the danger of lies and tries to cheer him up about his feelings of being 'common'.

Pip's humiliation by Estella prompts him to try to better himself and he asks Biddy to teach him all she knows. At the village inn, Pip finds Joe and Mr Wopsle talking to a stranger. This 'secret-looking man' *(Volume 1, Chapter 10)* shows great interest in Pip and signals to him, when the others are not looking, by rubbing his leg and then stirring his rum with the file that Pip recognizes as Joe's. Pip concludes that he **'knew my convict'** *(Volume 1, Chapter 10)*. The stranger gives Pip a shilling wrapped up in two pound notes.

- Joe's warning to Pip to tell no more lies once more associates him with Christian virtues opposed to **"the father of lies"** *(Volume 1, Chapter 9)*, the Devil.
- Chapter 9 ends with a direct address to readers to reflect on moments in their own lives, highlighting the significance of this 'turning point' in Pip's. He decides to embark on a programme of self-improvement – a theme in the novel.
- The appearance of a messenger from Magwitch disturbs Pip, who feels contaminated by his association with the criminal world.

> **Key quotations**
>
> That was a memorable day to me, for it made great changes in me. But it is the same with any life. Imagine one selected day struck out of it, and think how different its course would have been. Pause you who read this, and think for a moment of the long chain of iron or gold, of thorns or flowers, that would never have bound you, but for the formation of the first link on one memorable day. *(Volume 1, Chapter 9)*

Activity 4

Why do you think Pip made up the specific lies that he did? Is there any relationship between his true experience at Satis House and the false one that he concocts? Try and find some links between them and then share them with your class.

Volume 1, Chapters 11 and 12

Pip returns to Satis House where some of Miss Havisham's **'toady'** relations have gathered for her birthday (Volume 1, Chapter 11). Miss Havisham puts Pip to 'work', walking her around the disused dining room, where her bridal cake from many years ago still lies rotting, infested with spiders and mice and beetles. She explains that when she is laid out dead on the top table where the cake stands in decay, it will be **'the finished curse'** *(Volume 1, Chapter 11)* on the man who jilted her. Pip meets a mysterious looking gentleman descending the stairs, who tells Pip to behave himself. He also meets a **'pale young gentleman'** *(Volume 1, Chapter 11)*, who challenges him to a boxing contest, which Pip, surprisingly, wins. Estella rewards him with a kiss.

Pip feels guilty about having beaten his boxing opponent. At Miss Havisham's request, Pip visits her on alternate days. One day, Miss Havisham decides to summon Joe Gargery so that Pip may be apprenticed.

Miss Havisham's bridal banquet lies rotting amongst the spiders' webs

- Pip meets both Jaggers and Herbert Pocket at Miss Havisham's house, which strengthens his belief, later on, that Miss Havisham is his secret **benefactor**.
- The decaying wedding cake is a visible symbol of Miss Havisham's own life, which she has wasted, shut up in the gloom of Satis House.
- Pip's defeat of the 'pale young gentleman' is yet another source of guilt for Pip. The words 'guilt' and 'guilty' are repeated throughout the novel, supporting the theme.

benefactor a supporter with good intentions; in this novel, the word implies financial support

toady a false flatterer

Key quotations

He seemed so brave and innocent, that although I had not proposed the contest I felt but a gloomy satisfaction in my victory. Indeed, I go so far as to hope that I regarded myself while dressing, as a species of savage young wolf or other wild beast. (*Volume 1, Chapter 12*)

I enlarged upon my knowing nothing and wanting to know everything, in the hope that she might offer some help towards that desirable end. But she did not; on the contrary, she seemed to prefer my being ignorant. (*Volume 1, Chapter 12*)

Activity 5

Pip's boxing match is the second fight of the novel; the first was between the two escaped convicts. Re-read the description of both fights and then write a paragraph to explain the differences between the ferocious struggle between the convicts and the more formal boxing bout played according to rules.

Volume 1, Chapters 13 and 14

Miss Havisham presents Joe with 25 guineas as a premium that Pip **"has earned"** and she tells him to expect **"no more"** *(Volume 1, Chapter 13)*. Pip is acutely embarrassed by Joe, who addresses all his answers to Miss Havisham's questions to Pip. Pip is bound as an apprentice and Mrs Joe invites Pumblechook, the Hubbles and Wopsle to a celebratory meal, which Pip must endure.

The older, wiser Pip looks back at his unhappiness during his apprenticeship. He recognizes that Joe's almost saintly qualities and moral decency kept him from running away to be a sailor or soldier. His unhappiness stemmed from the realization that he and Estella came from such different backgrounds that they could never be together.

- Miss Havisham sees the goodness in Joe, despite Pip's embarrassment.
- Miss Havisham is adamant that Pip should not return nor expect more from her.
- The word 'bound', along with other images of capture, is frequent in the novel.

Key quotations

I remember that when I got into my little bedroom I was truly wretched, and had a strong conviction on me that I should never like Joe's trade. I had liked it once, but once was not now. *(Volume 1, Chapter 13)*

I was quite as dejected on the first working-day of my apprenticeship as in that after-time; but I am glad to know that I never breathed a murmur to Joe while my **indentures** lasted. It is about the only thing I *am* glad to know of myself in that connexion. *(Volume 1, Chapter 14)*

Activity 6

The mature voice of Pip, the narrator, becomes increasingly harsh in relation to the obnoxious Pumblechook and increasingly full of admiration in relation to Joe in these chapters. Re-read them and make a note of the contrasting language used to describe the two men. What effect do you think Dickens is intending here?

Volume 1, Chapters 15–17

Pip asks Joe for a half-day holiday from the forge to visit Miss Havisham. Mrs Joe is outraged when Joe agrees, giving his **journeyman**, Orlick, a holiday too. An angry row breaks out and Orlick calls Mrs Joe a **"foul shrew"** *(Volume 1, Chapter 15)*. She forces Joe to challenge Orlick to a fight, which Joe easily wins. At Satis House, Miss Havisham tells Pip that Estella is abroad and taunts him: **"Do you feel that you have lost her?"** *(Volume 1, Chapter 15)* On his way home, Pip meets Orlick, also heading to the forge, where they find that Mrs Joe has been attacked by an intruder and left for dead.

Pip feels guilty that, unknowingly, he provided Mrs Joe's attacker with his weapon – the filed leg-iron from his convict. Biddy comes to the forge to care for Mrs Joe. Pip suspects that Orlick attacked his sister, but Mrs Joe appears pleased to see him.

Pip confides in Biddy about his admiration for Estella and ambition to be a gentleman. Biddy suggests that Estella's opinion of Pip as 'coarse and common' was **"neither a very true nor a very polite thing to say"** *(Volume 1, Chapter 17)*. Pip seems to have confused feelings for Biddy. Pip visits Miss Havisham annually, on his birthday, when she gives him a guinea.

- Miss Havisham's initial reception of Pip (**"I hope you want nothing? You'll get nothing"** *Volume 1, Chapter 15*) is not that of a benefactor.
- Pip is once more touched by crime; the police are incompetent and Orlick is not arrested.
- Pip compares Biddy with Estella and recognizes that he could have a future life with Biddy, if only he could conquer his feelings for Estella.

indentures the contract made between an apprentice and his employer

journeyman a fully trained worker in a craft or trade, employed/paid by the day

Key quotations

It was horrible to think that I had provided the weapon, however undesignedly, but I could hardly think otherwise. I suffered unspeakable trouble while I considered and reconsidered whether I should at last dissolve that spell of my childhood, and tell Joe all the story. *(Volume 1, Chapter 16)*

Imperceptibly I became conscious of a change in Biddy... She was not beautiful—she was common, and could not be like Estella—but she was pleasant and wholesome and sweet-tempered. *(Volume 1, Chapter 17)*

Activity 7

1. Do you think Pip is right or wrong to withhold valuable evidence about the crime against his sister? Write your arguments in two columns headed 'Right' and 'Wrong'.

2. Find the first description of Biddy in Chapter 7. How has she improved since then?

3. If you were a friend of Pip's at this point in his story, what advice would you give him about his 'love life', and why? Refer to examples from the text to support your ideas.

Volume 1, Chapters 18 and 19

Jaggers brings the news that Pip has "great expectations" *(Volume 1, Chapter 18)* provided that he retains the name of Pip and makes no enquiries about the identity of his benefactor. Pip believes it is Miss Havisham. After Jaggers' departure, Pip, Joe and Biddy are in a state of shock. Pip goes to bed, feeling the loneliest he has ever felt but he is cheered by the sight of wreaths of smoke from Joe's pipe, interpreting them as a 'blessing from Joe' *(Volume 1, Chapter 18)*.

Pip promises Joe that he will never forget him. Privately, Pip asks Biddy to do what she can to help Joe on "in his learning and his manners" *(Volume 1, Chapter 19)*. Biddy is indignant on Joe's behalf, but Pip accuses her of jealousy. Pip goes into town to order new clothes and Pumblechook treats him to a meal and **obsequiously** insists on repeatedly shaking his hands. Pip says goodbye to Miss Havisham, who allows him to believe that she is his 'fairy godmother' *(Volume 1, Chapter 19)*. Pip's only thoughts about the convict are that he is 'a long way off' and probably dead *(Volume 1, Chapter 19)*.

A miserable final evening is spent at the forge and Pip leaves early for the morning coach. He declines Joe's offer to walk with him to the coach, but regrets it as he walks alone, stopping to weep at the finger-post at the end of the village.

- Mr Jaggers is paid to be Pip's guardian and this relationship is based solely on money rather than blood ties or affection. The older Pip reflects on Joe's tenderness towards him and recognizes his own faults of ingratitude.

- Within hours of being told he is to be a gentleman, Pip begins to act with a sense of superiority towards Joe and Biddy, repeating Estella's insulting words of "coarse and common" *(Volume 1, Chapter 17)*.

- Pip is amazed by his first 'experience of the stupendous power of money' *(Volume 1, Chapter 19)* as he is flattered first by Mr Trabb and then by Uncle Pumblechook.

- The closing line of Chapter 19, 'And the mists had all solemnly risen now, and the world lay spread before me', echoes Milton's famous poem 'Paradise Lost'.

obsequious grovelling; excessively flattering

Key facts about 'Paradise Lost'

Paradise Lost is an epic poem written by John Milton in the 17th century. It tells the story of the temptation of Adam and Eve by Satan, and their subsequent banishment from the Garden of Eden.

Key quotations

I have often thought of him [Joe] since, like the steam-hammer, that can crush a man or pat an egg-shell, in his combination of strength with gentleness. *(Volume 1, Chapter 18)*

Activity 8

Look again at the role of the narrator in Chapter 19 and pick out as many examples as you can of the older Pip's criticisms of his younger self.

Volume 2, Chapter 20

Pip arrives at Jaggers' office in London to find that his guardian is out. Disturbed by the 'gaze' of two death casts, Pip takes a walk and finds himself amongst the **'fat and blood and foam'** *(Volume 2, Chapter 20)* of Smithfield meat market, which so nauseates him that he walks on to Newgate prison. Here he is shown the gallows and the site of other public punishments. Pip meets Jaggers in the street, surrounded by a variety of dubious clients, all clamouring for his attention. Back

Jaggers's environment, with its death casts and criminals, unnerves Pip

in the office, Jaggers explains that Pip will receive a regular and generous amount of money from his unnamed benefactor, then sends him to 'Barnard's Inn' where Pip is to spend the weekend with Herbert Pocket.

- Pip's first taste of his new life brings him into contact with criminals and with the ugly side of the law.
- Pip is impressed by the reputation and apparent power of his new guardian.

Key facts about Victorian fascination with criminals

Plaster casts of executed criminals were regularly made and exhibited at Newgate prison and at Madame Tussaud's waxworks. Copies could be bought by the general public.

Key quotations

... he was so good as to take me into a yard and show me where the gallows was kept, and also where people were publicly whipped, and then he showed me the Debtors' Door, out of which culprits came to be hanged... This was horrible, and gave me a sickening idea of London... *(Volume 2, Chapter 20)*

Activity 9

Go back through the chapter, looking for examples of Pip's very unpleasant first impressions of London. Discuss the effects that Dickens is aiming for in his vivid descriptions of the darker side of London.

Volume 2, Chapters 21 and 22

Mr Wemmick takes Pip to Herbert Pocket's lodgings – a dismal set of buildings suffering from decay and neglect. When Herbert arrives, Pip is amazed to discover that he is the young man he fought with at Satis House.

At Pip's request, Herbert corrects Pip's table manners. He explains how Miss Havisham was jilted on her wedding day by a man who worked for Miss Havisham's jealous half-brother. Between them, they had swindled a lot of money out of Miss Havisham.

Pip and Herbert are soon firm friends. Herbert reveals his ambitions to become an insurer of ships and the pair exchange confidences. They agree never to discuss Pip's benefactor, although, like everyone else, Herbert assumes it is Miss Havisham. Herbert takes Pip to his family home, where Pip is to be tutored by Matthew Pocket. Here he finds the Pocket family of seven children **'tumbling up'** *(Volume 2, Chapter 22)* under the distinctly unwatchful eye of their self-obsessed mother.

- Herbert is a gentleman in manners and appearance, despite claiming to be poor. He explains his father's views on what makes a gentleman, a key theme in the novel.

- The Pocket children 'tumble up' in contrast to Pip's being brought up 'by hand'. How children are brought up is also a key theme.

Key quotations

"… I have heard my father mention that he was a showyman, and the kind of man for the purpose. But that he was not to be, without ignorance or prejudice, mistaken for a gentleman, my father most strongly **asseverates**; because it is a principle of his that no man who was not a true gentleman at heart ever was, since the world began, a true gentleman in manner." *(Volume 2, Chapter 22)*

asseverate to insist seriously

tumble up suggests a childhood with little guidance and many accidents

Volume 2, Chapters 23–25

Pip settles in at Matthew Pocket's house and meets fellow students, Startop and Bentley Drummle. Over dinner, he discovers that Mrs Pocket spends all her time reading about the aristocracy and neglecting her children completely, whereas Pip finds Matthew Pocket to be a diligent and admirable tutor.

In Little Britain, Jaggers quizzes Pip about his expenses and Wemmick gives Pip a tour of the law practice. He describes Jaggers as a skilful lawyer, and "Deep… as Australia" *(Volume 2, Chapter 24)*. Wemmick invites Pip to his home in Walworth and advises him, when he goes to Jaggers' house, to look at his housekeeper who is 'a wild beast tamed' *(Volume 2, Chapter 24)*.

Pip visits Wemmick's little house, modified to appear like a little castle, complete with drawbridge. There, Wemmick cares tenderly for his father, the Aged P. Wemmick explains his philosophy about keeping the castle and the office separate.

- Mrs Pocket's obsession with rank and titles contributes to Dickens's exploration of class and what makes a truly noble character.
- Pip has several role models' in his new life – Jaggers, Wemmick, Matthew and Herbert Pocket – all of whom influence his developing character.
- Wemmick's relationship with his 'Aged P' is a touching one and suggests that Wemmick has received good parenting from his father (a key theme), which he repays both dutifully and lovingly.

Key quotations

…I said to Wemmick that I hardly knew what to make of Mr. Jaggers's manner… "Always seems to me," said Wemmick, "as if he had set a man-trap and was watching it. Suddenly—click—you're caught!" *(Volume 2, Chapter 24)*

"No; the office is one thing, and private life is another. When I go into the office, I leave the Castle behind me, and when I come into the Castle, I leave the office behind me." *(Volume 2, Chapter 25)*

Activity 10

Look back at the descriptions that Dickens has given of Jaggers so far in Volume 1, Chapters 11 and 18, and Volume 2, Chapter 20, as well as in this chapter. What impression have you formed of Jaggers so far? Make notes on his physical appearance, his mannerisms and the substance of what he says, as well as the ways in which he talks to people.

Volume 2, Chapter 26

Jaggers invites Pip, Herbert, Drummle and Startop to dinner at his home. Jaggers seems fascinated by Drummle, calling him **'the Spider'** *(Volume 2, Chapter 28)*, and appears to enjoy watching the young men bickering and competing for who is the strongest amongst them. Jaggers forces his housekeeper, Molly, to display her wrists, which are muscular and scarred, and which Jaggers pronounces the strongest that he has ever seen.

- Pip is disturbed by the appearance of the housekeeper, who reminds him of a witch.

- The word 'trap' is used again in this chapter in relation to Jaggers, alerting the reader to some danger lurking behind his mysterious character.

> **Key quotations**
>
> **Suddenly, he clapped his large hand on the housekeeper's like a trap... "If you talk of strength," said Mr. Jaggers, "I'll show you a wrist. Molly, let them see your wrist."** *(Volume 2, Chapter 26)*

Activity 11

Food, drink and meal times feature a great deal in the novel. Try to remember all the 'meals' that have been described so far. Write a paragraph describing the effects you think Dickens is trying to create through his references to food and eating. You may like to consider:

- what meal it is: breakfast, lunch, dinner, snack or celebration

- who is present at the meal

- where the meal is served

- what food and drink are served

- table manners.

Work in small groups to collect your evidence and then discuss your findings with the whole class.

Volume 2, Chapters 27 and 28

Joe visits Pip at his lodgings in London. Pip is embarrassed by Joe's awkward behaviour in his 'gentlemanly' presence and is unable to relax, while Herbert does all he can to make Joe feel comfortable. Joe delivers a message from Miss Havisham that Estella has returned from abroad and would like to see Pip. Before he leaves, Joe tells Pip, "I'm wrong in these clothes... You won't find half so much fault in me if you think of me in my forge dress, with my hammer in my hand, or even my pipe." Pip rushes out after him, 'but he was gone' (Volume 2, Chapter 27).

Pip sets off for Satis House the next day and is alarmed when two convicts board the same coach on their journey to the Hulks. One of them is the 'secret-looking man' (Volume 1, Chapter 10) he met at the Three Jolly Bargemen. On the journey, Pip overhears him telling the other convict about when "a **Lifer**" asked him to deliver money to "that boy that had fed him and kep his secret" (Volume 2, Chapter 28). Pip is filled with an 'undefined and vague' fear (Volume 2, Chapter 28). At the Blue Boar he reads an old newspaper article attributing his rise in fortune to Pumblechook.

- Joe's parting words to Pip reveal a real wisdom about life that is sometimes concealed beneath his 'simple' exterior. The older 'Pip' is becoming increasingly critical of the snobbishness of his younger self as the narrative develops.

- Pip's sudden surge of guilt after Joe's dignified exit is similar to the feelings of regret he had when he chose to leave the forge alone. Guilt is a key theme.

- In the coach, Pip experiences a 'dread' that made him 'tremble' (Volume 2, Chapter 28) when he hears about 'his' convict's determination to reward him. This could be a premonition about the origin of his 'expectations'.

Key quotations

"Pip, dear old chap, life is made of ever so many partings welded together, as I may say, and one man's a blacksmith, and one's a whitesmith, and one's a goldsmith, and one's a coppersmith. Diwisions among such must come, and must be met as they come. If there's been any fault at all to-day, it's mine. You and me is not two figures to be together in London..." (Volume 2, Chapter 27)

The great numbers on their backs, as if they were street doors; their coarse **mangy** ungainly outer surface, as if they were lower animals; their ironed legs, apologetically garlanded with pocket-handkerchiefs; and the way in which all present looked at them and kept from them; made them... a most disagreeable and degraded spectacle. (Volume 2, Chapter 28)

Lifer a criminal transported to Australia for life

mangy suggests both messy and dirty

Activity 12

Dickens is criticizing a 'justice' system that treats human beings like this – with no dignity. What other evidence can you find in the novel so far that suggests that Dickens thinks little of the way 'justice' operates in England in the early 1800s? Look again at Volume 1, Chapters 1, 3, 6, 10 and 16, and Volume 2, Chapter 20.

Volume 2, Chapters 29 and 30

Pip spends his morning fantasizing about Miss Havisham's intentions for him. He arrives at Satis House to find Orlick employed as a gate-keeper.

Pip does not immediately recognize Estella, who has grown lovelier than before. In a walk around the gardens together, Estella confesses that she has no heart, **'no softness'** *(Volume 2, Chapter 29)* and Pip is struck by her likeness to someone else, but he cannot fathom who. Jaggers arrives on business and spends the evening. It is agreed that when Estella comes to London, Pip will meet her.

Pip spends another broken night at the Blue Boar dreaming of his 'destiny' to marry Estella and, for her sake, decides to return to London without visiting Joe.

Estella treats Pip as her 'page'

Pip has Orlick dismissed from his position 'of trust' at Miss Havisham's *(Volume 2, Chapter 30)*. Later, Pip is mocked in the street by Trabb's boy, for his snobbishness. Pip sends Trabb a pompous note threatening to withdraw his custom because of the boy's impudence. In a heart-to-heart with Herbert, Pip confesses his love for Estella and Herbert tries to persuade Pip to **'detach'** *(Volume 2, Chapter 30)* himself from her. He tells Pip about Clara.

- Pip sees himself as a Prince Charming figure, selected by Miss Havisham to **'marry the Princess'** *(Volume 2, Chapter 29)*. In reality, the situation is very different; Estella seems more remote than ever and Miss Havisham seems slightly more deranged, manically urging Pip to love Estella.

- In one day, Pip is responsible for two lower-class characters losing their jobs. While he may be forgiven as regards Orlick, who he suspects of attacking Mrs Joe, his objection to Trabb's boy is based solely on his own wounded pride.

- His treatment of both Joe and Trabb's boy show him to be no gentleman yet.

> **Key quotations**
>
> "Hear me, Pip! I adopted her to be loved. I bred her and educated her, to be loved... Love her!"
>
> She said the word often enough, and there could be no doubt that she meant to say it; but if the often repeated word had been hate instead of love—despair—revenge—dire death—it could not have sounded from her lips more like a curse. *(Volume 2, Chapter 29)*

> **Activity 13**
>
> Despite Pip's recognition that Estella is not **'human perfection'** *(Volume 2, Chapter 29)*, he continues to love and worship her. Why do you think this is? Think of three possible reasons for his infatuation with her, then share your ideas as a class.

Volume 2, Chapters 31–33

Pip and Herbert go to the theatre to see Mr Wopsle's amateurish and comical performance in the lead role in *Hamlet*. Later, Pip's fevered dreams revolve around him acting the part of Hamlet in front of a huge audience without knowing his lines.

While waiting to meet Estella off the coach to London, Pip meets Wemmick and goes with him on a visit to Newgate prison. Wemmick's role in the prison reminds Pip of a gardener tending his plants – the prisoners who depend upon Jaggers for their survival. Pip describes Newgate at visiting time as an **'ugly, disorderly, depressing scene'** *(Volume 2, Chapter 32)*.

Pip tries to shake off the 'Newgate' air before meeting Estella. As the coach pulls in and he sees Estella waving to him, Pip experiences, for the second time, a sensation of a **'nameless shadow'** *(Volume 2, Chapter 32)* that he cannot grasp. This experience is repeated when Pip accompanies Estella in a carriage to Mrs Brandley's house in Richmond.

Pip is enchanted by Estella even though she tells Pip how all Matthew Pocket's relatives conspire to blacken his name with Miss Havisham, a fact which Estella finds immensely funny.

- Wopsle's transformation from church clerk to actor may be intended to parody Pip's change from blacksmith to gentleman, each of them appearing in 'costume' to represent something that they are really not.
- Pip witnesses Wemmick's popularity in the prison and begins to understand that all his mourning rings and brooches have come from Jaggers' clients who have been given the death penalty.
- Estella and Pip are being treated like puppets, acting out the wishes of others. Estella's laughter at Pip's concern for Miss Havisham's good opinion suggests that she knows full well that Miss Havisham is not Pip's benefactor.

Key facts about Victorian bereavement

In the nineteenth century, bereaved husbands, wives and children often wore mourning rings or brooches to commemorate their dead loved ones. These would usually be rings or brooches set with jet, stones or carved ivory, inscribed with the name, date of death and age of the deceased. Some of these would be of great value, others less so. Wemmick considers any such item to be "portable property" *(Volume 2, Chapter 24)* and therefore worth having.

Key quotations

Miserably I went to bed after all, and miserably thought of Estella, and miserably dreamed that my expectations were all cancelled, and that I had to give my hand in marriage to Herbert's Clara, or play Hamlet to Miss Havisham's Ghost, before twenty thousand people, without knowing twenty words of it. *(Volume 2, Chapter 31)*

Activity 14

Details of Pip's dreams, or of his bedtime thoughts, appear throughout the novel. As a class activity, find each example and discuss what you think they add to the story. In most cases, the details come at the end of the chapter; look at Chapters 2, 7, 9, 10, 13, 18 and 19 in Volume 1 and Chapters 29, 31, 35, 37 and 39 in Volume 2.

Volume 2, Chapters 34 and 35

The older Pip describes his idle way of life as he approaches his 21st birthday. He and Herbert have developed extravagant habits and both have mounting debts. One evening, when they are puzzling through their accounts, a letter arrives for Pip announcing the death of Mrs Joe.

Pip returns to the forge to attend his sister's funeral. That night, Joe, Biddy and Pip share a meal together and Pip promises Joe that he will visit often. In a private conversation, Biddy tells Pip how, before she died, Mrs Joe appeared to be asking for forgiveness over her unfair treatment of Joe and Pip. Biddy offends Pip by appearing to doubt his intentions to be a more regular visitor at the forge.

- Pip spends money freely on luxuries such as fine furniture, clothes and jewellery, which make him feel more like a gentleman.
- The mature narrator reveals that Biddy had been right to doubt his sincerity when he promised to visit Joe more regularly.

> **Key quotations**
>
> Once more, the mists were rising as I walked away. If they disclosed to me, as I suspect they did, that I should not come back, and that Biddy was quite right, all I can say is, —they were quite right too. *(Volume 2, Chapter 35)*

> **Activity 15**
>
> Chapter 35 describes Mrs Joe's funeral and yet the early part of the chapter is largely comical. How does Dickens create this comedy? You should look at the comic descriptions of the funeral directors and mourners as well as the actions of the bystanders.

Volume 2, Chapters 36 and 37

Pip comes of age and Mr Jaggers reveals that he is to be paid a regular yearly allowance of £500 until his patron chooses to come forward. Pip seeks advice from Wemmick about using some of his money to help Herbert to make a start in business. Wemmick's 'official' response is that he may as well throw his money in the Thames as invest in a friend. Pip resolves to visit Wemmick in Walworth to hear his **"Walworth sentiments"** *(Volume 2, Chapter 36).*

Pip makes 'a **pilgrimage**' *(Volume 2, Chapter 37)* to Walworth and learns more about Wemmick from the Aged P. He also meets Wemmick's lady friend, Miss Skiffins. Wemmick agrees to assist Pip in his plan to purchase Herbert 'an opening' to a partnership with a young shipping insurer named Clarriker. The whole business is to be arranged without Herbert's knowledge.

- Wemmick's ability to keep the office and the 'castle' separate allows him to work amongst criminals during the day without allowing unpleasant cases to spoil his home life.
- Pip becomes Herbert's secret benefactor and takes great pleasure in doing **'some good'** *(Volume 2, Chapter 37)* with his 'expectations'.

> **pilgrimage** a journey made to a 'sacred' or 'holy' place with the intention of becoming a better person; here the word is a metaphor for Pip's journey and moral progress

> **Key quotations**
>
> "Take a chair, Mr. Pip," said my guardian.
>
> As I sat down, and he preserved his attitude and bent his brows at his boots, I felt at a disadvantage, which reminded me of that old time when I had been put upon a tombstone. *(Volume 2, Chapter 36)*

Activity 16

1. Why do you think Dickens chooses this moment to recall Pip's meeting with the convict on the marshes?

2. It is often suggested that Pip's 'journey' in the novel is similar to that of the character of 'Christian' in John Bunyan's *A Pilgrim's Progress*. In pairs, do some Internet research into this book and pick out some similarities based on plot outlines that you find.

Volume 2, Chapters 38 and 39

Pip describes the agony he endured watching Estella flirting with other men at dances, parties and excursions. At Satis House, he witnesses a fierce quarrel between Estella and Miss Havisham, who reproaches Estella for being **"cold"** to her *(Volume 2, Chapter 38)*. Back in his London club, Pip challenges Bentley Drummle to a duel for insolently drinking to the health of Estella but has to withdraw the challenge when Estella confirms that she and Drummle know each other.

One night, Pip is disturbed by the sound of footsteps on the staircase. He opens the door to a stranger who turns out to be 'his' convict. Magwitch greets Pip warmly, holding out his hands to him, although Pip is repulsed by his appearance and familiarity. Gradually, Magwitch reveals that he is Pip's secret benefactor. In complete shock, Pip's treatment of Magwitch is snobbish and ungentlemanly, but Magwitch does not reproach him.

- Chapter 38 ends with an ominous reference to an **'Eastern story'** about the crushing of the Sultan's enemies under a **'heavy slab'**, foreshadowing the crushing of Pip's dreams when his real benefactor is revealed.

- Magwitch tells Pip, **"I'm your second father"** *(Volume 2, Chapter 39)*, linking to the theme of parenting.

- Pip claims that the **'sharpest and deepest pain of all'** was that it was for this convict that he had **'deserted Joe'** *(Volume 2, Chapter 39)*.

Key quotations

"Yes, Pip, dear boy, I've made a gentleman on you! It's me wot has done it! I swore that time, sure as ever I earned a guinea, that guinea should go to you. I swore arterwards, sure as ever I spec'lated and got rich, you should get rich. I lived rough, that you should live smooth; I worked hard, that you should be above work." *(Volume 2, Chapter 39)*

Activity 17

1. In groups of three and taking the parts of Pip, Magwitch and the narrator, read this highly dramatic chapter aloud from 'There is someone down there is there not?' to the end.

2. Then make a list of adjectives to describe Pip's feelings about Magwitch's revelation and another to describe Magwitch's feelings as he is finally reunited with 'his' boy.

3. What is it about Magwitch that Pip finds so repulsive? In pairs, consider Pip's feelings and make a list of the things that Pip objects to.

Volume 3, Chapters 40–42

Pip decides to tell people that 'Provis' (Magwitch) is his uncle. He buys clothes to disguise him and takes rooms for him nearby. Pip visits Jaggers, who confirms that Magwitch is Pip's sole benefactor and that there was **'Not a particle of evidence'** *(Volume 3, Chapter 40)* to suggest that it was Miss Havisham. Pip is disgusted by everything about the convict, including his coarse table manners and his sense of possessing Pip. Magwitch revels in the fact that he has made a gentleman of Pip. When Herbert returns, Magwitch makes him swear to secrecy on the Bible.

Pip tries to disguise Magwitch in new clothes, trying to make the convict look more like his benefactor

Herbert shares Pip's repugnance at Magwitch's manners and understands Pip's decision not to accept any more of his money. Ironically, Herbert suggests that Pip might work at Clarriker's, where he is doing well, little suspecting **'with whose money'** *(Volume 3, Chapter 41)*. Herbert warns Pip that Magwitch might give himself up to the authorities if Pip simply abandons him and together they agree that Pip must persuade Magwitch to go abroad with him.

Magwitch tells Pip and Herbert his miserable story about a life spent in and out of jails and of his criminal involvement with Compeyson. He explains his bitterness over Compeyson's more lenient jail sentence based on his appearance as a gentleman. Herbert tells Pip that Compeyson was the man who broke Miss Havisham's heart.

- Just as Miss Havisham has raised Estella to take revenge on the male sex, Magwitch intends to watch Pip spending his money to get back at the judges and colonists who have harmed him. Both Pip and Estella are victims of the whims of their patrons.

- Herbert proves himself to be a true friend to Pip.

- Magwitch's progress in life as a defenceless orphan offers a glimpse into what Pip might have become without the shelter and love that Joe gave him at the forge.

Key quotations

"And when the verdict come, warn't it Compeyson as was recommended to mercy on account of good character and bad company, and giving up all the information he could agen me, and warn't it me as got never a word but Guilty?" *(Volume 3, Chapter 42)*

Activity 18

Does Magwitch's life story change your perceptions of this 'hardened' criminal? What effects does Dickens achieve by allowing Magwitch to tell his own story? Consider the language and speech patterns that he uses.

Volume 3, Chapters 43–46

Pip decides to see Estella and Miss Havisham before going abroad with Magwitch. He finds Bentley Drummle staying at the Blue Boar. Coming on top of his discovery that Miss Havisham is not his benefactor, Bentley Drummle's presence at the Blue Boar suggests that Pip has no hope with Estella.

Miss Havisham admits that she has used Pip to torment her relations as well as to test Estella's potential to break men's hearts. Pip asks her to help Herbert Pocket to continue his career. Pip declares his love for Estella, but she explains that she is to marry Bentley Drummle and that she is incapable of love herself. Pip's utter wretchedness appears to touch Miss Havisham at last.

Pip returns to London but is stopped at Whitefriars gate by the night-porter with a message from Wemmick: 'DON'T GO HOME' *(Volume 3, Chapter 44)*. He spends a miserable night in a hotel worrying, then goes early to Walworth where Wemmick warns him that Compeyson is on Magwitch's trail. Magwitch has been moved to the relative safety of lodgings by the river, where Herbert's sweetheart Clara lives with her 'bedridden Pa' *(Volume 3, Chapter 45)*. Wemmick promises to let Pip know when it is safe to get Magwitch out of the country.

Pip visits Magwitch in his new lodgings. He meets Clara and hears the great noise made by her heavy-drinking, overbearing father, whom Herbert has nicknamed 'Gruffandgrim' *(Volume 3, Chapter 46)*. Pip believes that Magwitch has 'softened' *(Volume 3, Chapter 46)* and he parts from him with some regret. Pip buys a boat so that he and Herbert can row past the lodgings regularly, in training for getting Magwitch away by boat to board a steamer to the continent.

- Pip is broken-hearted by Estella's act of self-destruction in marrying Drummle. Miss Havisham's plan has backfired and Estella will suffer as much as she did herself.
- Wemmick urges Pip to get hold of Magwitch's **'portable property'** *(Volume 3, Chapter 45)*; materialism is very important in the novel.
- Pip sees a change in Magwitch, perhaps having heard his miserable life story and knowing that he is in mortal danger.

> **Key quotations**
>
> **I found Provis comfortably settled. He expressed no alarm, and seemed to feel none that was worth mentioning; but it struck me that he was softened—indefinably, for I could not have said how, and could never afterwards recall how when I tried; but certainly.** *(Volume 3, Chapter 46)*

Activity 19

In pairs, consider what Miss Havisham and Magwitch originally intended to achieve for Estella and Pip respectively, and compare this with the actual outcomes.

Volume 3, Chapters 47–49

Though deeply in debt, Pip refuses to touch any more of Magwitch's money. He attends another of Wopsle's performances at the theatre. After the show, Wopsle tells him that the convict with the mauled face (Compeyson) was sitting behind Pip all evening.

Pip is invited to dinner by Jaggers and Wemmick is also present. Jaggers discusses the likely mistreatment of Estella by Bentley Drummle, while Pip observes the mannerisms of Molly the housekeeper and concludes that she is Estella's mother. Wemmick privately reveals that Molly was acquitted of a murder charge through Jaggers' defence of her and that at the time Molly had a three-year-old daughter and had been married to a **'tramping man'** *(Volume 3, Chapter 48)*.

Pip visits Miss Havisham, who is full of remorse for the damage she has done to Estella and Pip. She begs Pip's forgiveness and agrees to supply the £900 necessary to complete the purchase of Herbert's partnership. Pip refuses her offer to give him money for himself. As Pip is about to leave Satis House, Miss Havisham's dress catches fire and Pip rescues her, smothering the flames with his greatcoat. His hands are burnt but he saves her life.

- Wopsle's ambitions as an actor have come to nothing. There are some similarities between Wopsle's and Pip's 'expectations' as both are dashed.
- Pieces of the puzzle about Estella's parents are beginning to fall into place.

- Pip's forgiveness of Miss Havisham is a Christian virtue.
- Miss Havisham's injuries are treated in a bed made up on the table where the bridal cake had been, as she prophesied in Volume 1, Chapter 11.

> **Key quotations**
>
> "My name is on the first leaf. If you can ever write under my name, 'I forgive her,' though ever so long after my broken heart is dust—pray do it!"
>
> "O Miss Havisham," said I, "I can do it now. There have been sore mistakes; and my life has been a blind and thankless one; and I want forgiveness and direction far too much, to be bitter with you."
> *(Volume 3, Chapter 49)*

Activity 20

As a class, identify how many acts of real goodness Pip performs in the course of his story.

Volume 3, Chapters 50–52

Herbert dresses Pip's burns and tells him more of what Magwitch has told him of his history. Pip realizes that Estella is Magwitch's child.

Pip is determined to have Estella's true parentage confirmed and he visits Jaggers, who for once appears to be taken by surprise. Jaggers eventually concedes that he placed Estella with Miss Havisham to offer the child an escape from a life that promised to be wretched. Jaggers, Wemmick and Pip all agree that no good would come of revealing the truth to any of the parties concerned.

Pip receives a message from Wemmick to say that Magwitch might be whisked abroad later in the week. Herbert and Pip enlist the help of Startop as a second rower, as Pip's arm is still very painful from the fire. When Pip gets home, he finds a mysterious note urging him to go to the **limekiln** down on the marshes to learn something about his Uncle Provis. He goes at once.

- In his bartering for information from Jaggers, Pip reveals that Wemmick has an aged parent and a happy home life, to Jaggers' amazement.
- The puzzle is solved; the two halves of Pip's early experiences – the fantasy world of Satis House and the brutal world of convicts and crime – are fitted together.
- Pip's decision to go to the limekilns alone and to leave a misleading note for Herbert is a device to create maximum tension.

limekiln a place where quick lime, a chemical associated with the disposal of dead bodies, is made

Activity 21

Jaggers accuses Wemmick of playing a part, calling him **"the most cunning impostor in all London"** *(Volume 3, Chapter 51)*. Which other characters in the novel appear to be play-acting? Work in pairs.

Volume 3, Chapters 53–54

Pip arrives at the limekiln in the dark and is suddenly seized and bound by an unseen assailant, who turns out to be Orlick. Resentful of Pip since he was a child and bitter about his dismissal from Miss Havisham's, Orlick announces his intention to kill Pip and dump his body in the limekiln where it will never be found. Orlick admits to having been the man who attacked Mrs Joe and to have been trailing Magwitch since his arrival in England. Just as Orlick is about to strike, Herbert, Startop and Trabb's boy burst in and rescue Pip, although Orlick escapes.

Although Pip is shaken by his ordeal, he, Herbert and Startop pick up Magwitch as pre-arranged and make off down the river to pick up a steamer for the continent. Pip is fully committed to saving Magwitch from capture and finds him further softened and compliant as he sits peaceably in the boat. Just as the steamer bound for Hamburg comes into view, another boat appears out of nowhere, pulls alongside and Magwitch is denounced as a 'returned Transport' *(Volume 3, Chapter 54)*. Magwitch recognizes Compeyson, who has informed on him and he grapples him out of the boat. Magwitch surfaces, badly injured, having been hit by the ship's keel. Compeyson is drowned. Magwitch is arrested, but Pip is allowed to accompany him on his journey to Newgate prison.

Magwitch is recaptured at the last minute

- During Orlick's tormenting speeches in the limekiln, all Pip can think of is what his disappearance will mean to those he loves: Herbert, Joe, Biddy and even Magwitch, who will all think he has deserted them.

- The final struggle that ensues between Magwitch and Compeyson echoes their discovery on the marsh in Volume 1, Chapter 5, where they were fighting in a ditch.

- Pip has to surrender Magwitch's pocketbook, stuffed with money, which had once been in his possession.

> **Key quotations**
>
> For now, my repugnance to him had all melted away; and in the hunted, wounded, shackled creature who held my hand in his, I only saw a man who had meant to be my benefactor, and who had felt affectionately, gratefully, and generously, towards me with great constancy through a series of years. I only saw in him a much better man than I had been to Joe. *(Volume 3, Chapter 54)*

Volume 3, Chapters 55–56

Pip engages Jaggers to defend Magwitch, but his case is hopeless. Jaggers and Wemmick regret Pip's failure to save the 'portable property', but Pip's only concern is that Magwitch still believes that his legacy is safe. Herbert's work takes him to Cairo and Pip agrees to consider joining him there as a clerk after Magwitch's certain death and his own resolution of 'a vague something lingering in my thoughts' *(Volume 3, Chapter 55)*. Wemmick invites Pip to take a walk that turns into his wedding to Miss Skiffins; the Aged P gives the bride away.

Magwitch is tried, found guilty and sentenced to death. Pip visits him daily, holding his hand and speaking gently to him. By night, he writes letters to prominent people, including the Home Secretary, asking for a pardon for his benefactor. The injuries that Magwitch sustained on the river are fatal and he is very weak when Pip discloses to him that the little daughter, who he thought lost, is alive, is a lady, and is loved by Pip. Magwitch presses Pip's hand to his lips and dies contentedly. Pip offers a prayer for God's forgiveness.

- Pip's one good deed with his expectations has turned out to be a blessing to him. He also has the prospect of respectable employment with Herbert.

- Pip has repaid Magwitch's loyalty and has 'redeemed' himself.

Key facts about the concept of redemption

In Christian teaching, Jesus redeemed or saved the souls of all humanity when he died on the cross for their sins. Here, Pip makes up for his negative feelings about Magwitch when he first discovered that he was his benefactor by now caring for him, sincerely, until his death.

> **Key quotations**
>
> Rising for a moment, a distinct speck of face in this way of light, the prisoner said, "My Lord, I have received my sentence of Death from the Almighty, but I bow to yours," and sat down again. *(Volume 3, Chapter 56)*

> **Activity 22**
>
> Magwitch responds in a very dignified way to the judge's death sentence. What do you think Dickens's attitude towards the death penalty is, as represented in this chapter?

Volume 3, Chapters 57–58

After Magwitch's death, Pip is deeply in debt and falls gravely ill. As he begins to recover, he realizes that it is Joe who has come to nurse him better. Joe and Pip are reconciled as the 'best of friends', as they were when Pip was a little boy. Joe doesn't let Pip dwell on the past and, when he senses that Pip is strong enough to do without him, he leaves London without notice, enclosing in a dignified note, the receipts for Pip's debts, which he has settled. Pip resolves to return to the forge, seek Joe's forgiveness and ask Biddy to marry him.

Pip returns to the Blue Boar where Pumblechook accuses him of ingratitude. Pip is rude in his replies and hurries off, hoping to find Biddy in her schoolroom, but both the school and the forge are shut up. Pip has arrived on Biddy's wedding day to Joe and he expresses great pleasure in their evident happiness, relieved that he had not breathed a word of his intentions to Joe. Pip sincerely begs and receives forgiveness from both Joe and Biddy. He announces his intentions to go abroad and to settle his debts. In a summary of the later events of his life, Pip explains how he made progress from clerk to partner at Clarriker.

- Joe's faithful love towards Pip, his selfless payment of Pip's debts and hiscomplete forgiveness of Pip's lack of loyalty to him when he had his 'expectations' mark him out as the **"gentle Christian man"** *(Volume 3, Chapter 57)*, who Pip blesses as he recovers from his illness.

- Clarriker reveals Pip to be Herbert's benefactor when Pip is made partner in the firm. Herbert receives the news with great joy, in steep contrast to Pip's reception of similar news from Magwitch.

> **Key quotations**
>
> "... I shall never rest until I have worked for the money with which you have kept me out of prison, and have sent it to you, don't think, dear Joe and Biddy, that if I could repay it a thousand times over, I suppose I could cancel a farthing of the debt I owe you, or that I would do so if I could!" *(Volume 3, Chapter 58)*

Activity 23

Although Joe is a simple blacksmith, Dickens clearly intends the reader to see him as equal in gentility to any gentleman. In pairs, see how many occasions you can think of where Dickens invites his readers to consider what makes a real gentleman. You will find some useful references in Volume 1, Chapters 5, 17; Volume 2, Chapters 22, 39; and Volume 3, Chapters 40–44, 52 and 53.

Volume 3, Chapter 59

Eleven years after Pip went abroad, he returns to the forge and finds a little boy named Pip sitting by the fire. Biddy asks Pip if he still yearns for Estella, but he tells her that that **'poor dream... has all gone by'** (Volume 3, Chapter 59). Pip tells the reader of Estella's deep unhappiness and of the cruelty she suffered at the hands of Bentley Drummle. Later, Pip visits the ruins of Satis House and meets Estella, who is bidding farewell to the place where she spent her youth. Estella admits that she has changed and now understands the misery she caused Pip. They leave the place hand in hand.

- The ending of the novel is ambiguous and it is up to the reader to decide whether Pip and Estella are reunited for life or whether Pip is being optimistic in seeing no **'parting from her'** (Volume 3, Chapter 59).

Key quotations

I took her hand in mine, and we went out of the ruined place; and, as the morning mists had risen long ago when I first left the forge, so the evening mists were rising now, and in all the broad expanse of tranquil light they showed to me, I saw the shadow of no parting from her. (Volume 3, Chapter 59)

Activity 24

Do you believe that Pip and Estella will marry? Have a class debate to consider whether or not they are likely to 'live happily ever after'.

Structure

The structure of a novel is determined by the order in which the story is told as well as by the ways in which different points of view are presented within it. The structure is the result of careful shaping by the author, who must initially engage a reader's attention while introducing aspects of character, plot and theme. The writer must maintain the reader's interest while the plot develops to a climax through a series of crises, sensational events or reversals of fortune, finally gathering momentum and leading the reader to a satisfying conclusion.

In *Great Expectations*, Dickens engages our attention with the opening chapters involving Pip's frightening experience with the convicts and their capture (Volume 1, Chapters 1–6); the characters that make up Pip's childhood world are introduced and developed in Chapters 2–15, including his family and neighbours as well as Miss Havisham and Estella. Chapter 16 presents the sensational event of the attack on Mrs Joe, followed swiftly in Chapter 18 by the momentous news of Pip's 'expectations', maintaining our interest to the end of the first volume when Pip sets off to London and a new life.

Volume 2 follows a similar pattern, introducing and developing the London characters of Jaggers, Wemmick and the Aged P, the Pockets, Drummle and Startop, and maintaining interest in Pip's 'romance' with Estella as he travels between London and his home town to keep in touch with Miss Havisham. Dickens also maintains the reader's interest by introducing comic sections such as those that involve the Pocket children, Wopsle's abysmal performances in the theatre as Mr Waldengarver and Wemmick's charming attentions to his profoundly deaf Aged P. The climax of Volume 2 (and arguably of the whole book) is Magwitch's reappearance in the final chapter.

The final volume is structured similarly. Some new characters are introduced – Clara, her father and her landlady, Mrs Whimple. Pip is still travelling between London and Satis House, and we are still engaged by his pursuit of Estella, but now his need to get Magwitch to safety gives momentum to the story. Revelations about Estella's true parentage keep the readers hooked and Dickens does not fail to provide sensation, with Pip falling into Orlick's trap but being rescued at the last minute. The dash for freedom and crushing of Pip's and Magwitch's hopes, when Magwitch is arrested, also provide excitement for the reader. Dickens exploits the reader's sentimental responses both to Magwitch's death and to Pip's collapse. The reintroduction of Joe and his tender nursing of Pip after his reversal in fortune bring the novel towards its conclusion, although perhaps the ambiguity of the ending prevents it from being fully 'satisfying'.

Dickens wanted his novels to reach a wide audience and for this reason he published them in episodes or 'instalments' in cheap weekly magazines, each ending with a cliffhanger or hook to keep his readers coming back. *Great Expectations* was published in 36 weekly instalments made up of one long chapter or two shorter chapters.

Dickens did not write the complete novel and then publish it in serial form. He was a long way from reaching the end of writing before the first instalments were published. There are some advantages in writing like this, as Dickens was able to respond to his readers' reactions to certain characters.

Activity 25

With this structure in mind, create a chart to illustrate where key events occur in each volume.

Key facts about Victorian magazines

Instalments were relatively cheap to buy. *All the Year Round* cost two pence a week and had a subscription of between 100,000 and 300,000 regular readers, all looking forward to the next instalment, much like fans of TV 'soaps' today.

It is also possible to see the novel as being structured to conform to the Christian pattern of innocence (Volume 1), temptation/fall into sin (Volume 2) and **redemption/salvation** (Volume 3). This interpretation of the structure of the novel is supported by Dickens's numerous allusions to scripture as well as to the similarities to Bunyan's *A Pilgrim's Progress*. It is often suggested that Pip's 'journey' in the novel is similar to that of the character of 'Christian' in Bunyan's book.

 Activity 26

1. Write a paragraph about each of the volumes, suggesting ways in which they conform to this Christian pattern.

2. In pairs, do some Internet research into *A Pilgrim's Progress* and pick out some similarities based on plot outlines that you find.

redemption and salvation terms that refer to the belief in Christian teaching that people can be forgiven for their sins and live with God forever in heaven

Narrative viewpoint

Great Expectations is narrated in the **first person**, as if by the older Pip looking back over the significant events in his life. The story is presented in **chronological order**. Pip the little boy is presented largely sympathetically by his mature self, but as Pip grows up, the narrative voice becomes increasingly critical of his own youthful behaviour, especially in relation to his treatment of Joe. Sometimes the narrator addresses the reader directly, inviting us to reflect upon our own actions; sometimes he merely narrates events in Pip's life or recalls lengthy conversations from years before. Sometimes, the narrator makes way for individual characters to tell their own stories, in their own words, as when Magwitch relates his life story in Volume 3, Chapter 42.

The older Pip obviously has complete knowledge of the life that he recounts, but he chooses not to share this knowledge from the beginning, so that we are kept in the dark, for example, about who his real benefactor is and about who was lurking on the stairs when Magwitch showed up, and this increases the novel's suspense and the reader's anticipation of what is to come. The narrative gives us access to the perceptions of his former self (aged between 7 years at the beginning of the book to 34 years old at the end) as well as the perceptions of the older, wiser man, reflecting upon his past behaviour.

This kind of novel, in which the main character grows up and learns from his or her mistakes, is often called a 'coming of age' novel or **Bildungsroman**.

Key quotations

In the pantry, which was far more abundantly supplied than usual, owing to the season, I was very much alarmed by a hare hanging up by the heels, whom I rather thought I caught, when my back was half turned, winking. *(Volume 1, Chapter 2, while raiding the pantry as a child)*

Heaven knows we need never be ashamed of our tears, for they are rain upon the blinding dust of earth, overlying our hard hearts. I was better after I had cried than before—more sorry, more aware of my own ingratitude, more gentle. If I had cried before, I should have had Joe with me then. *(Volume 1, Chapter 19, reflecting, as an older, wiser man, on his tears as he left the village for London)*

Bildungsroman a novel about the early years of somebody's life, exploring the development of his or her character and personality

chronological order the order in which events happened, from the earliest to the latest

first person the use of the pronouns 'I' and 'me'. In a story written in the first person the narrator is usually telling a story in which he or she has a major role. Such a perspective allows intimate access to the narrator's thoughts but no access into the inner workings of the other characters

Writing about plot and structure

Upgrade

You need to know the plot of the novel in great detail, but remember that when you are writing in your assessment, you must show that you understand Dickens's methods, as well as knowing the plot, especially when you are answering questions based on an extract from the novel. You will be expected to comment upon:

- the structure of the novel and how Dickens builds and maintains the readers' interest
- Dickens's methods of creating character
- his methods of bringing out important themes
- his choice and use of language, imagery and motifs.

In your assessment, you may be asked to comment on the novel's structure. Think about the different effects that Dickens achieves by, for example:

- placing a very serious section next to a comical one
- making the revelations about Magwitch, Molly and their relationship to Estella slip out, one by one, like pieces in a puzzle, in Chapters 48 and 50 of Volume 3
- ending each instalment (rather than each chapter) on a cliffhanger: e.g. the end of Chapter 4 in Volume 1 has Pip running into **'a party of soldiers with their muskets'** at the door of the forge; the end of Chapter 15 in Volume 1 sees Mrs Joe lying senseless on the floor, **'knocked down by a tremendous blow'** from **'some unknown hand'**, while Volume 2 ends, in Chapter 39, with the revelation that Magwitch is Pip's benefactor
- moving the action between different settings, in London and Pip's home town, in Volumes 2 and 3, creating tension between Pip's old life and his 'new' one.

Biography of Charles Dickens

- Charles Dickens was born in Portsmouth in 1812.

- In 1824, his father was sent to the Marshalsea prison for debtors and Charles's education was abruptly halted. Charles was put to work in a sordid 'blacking' factory (like the one mentioned by Joe on his visit to Pip in Volume 2, Chapter 27), where his job was to stick labels on jars of boot polish. Dickens never forgot this humiliating experience. After his father was released, Dickens resumed his education.

Charles Dickens (1812–1870) was famous in his own lifetime and gave readings of his work to huge, enthusiastic crowds

- The adult Dickens first found employment as a parliamentary reporter. This allowed him to hear the parliamentary debates that shaped his concerns for the poor and the underprivileged, reflected both in his fiction and in the extensive charitable work that he undertook throughout his lifetime.

- Between 1836 and 1837, at the age of 24, Dickens published *The Pickwick Papers*, using the pseudonym 'Boz'. These stories became tremendously popular with the reading public. He became a major celebrity of his day and amassed a large personal fortune. His published fiction includes 15 major novels, 5 Christmas books and 6 'minor' works, including *A Child's History of England*.

- In the same year as his writing career took off, Dickens married Catherine Hogarth. They had ten children together but separated in 1858 at Dickens's insistence. There were rumours that Dickens was in love with a young actress named Ellen Ternan.

- Dickens wrote *Great Expectations* in 1860 and there has been speculation that Ellen was the inspiration for Pip's unattainable love, Estella.

- From 1858 until his death in 1870, Dickens made a series of tours of British towns and cities where he gave readings of his work to huge and enthusiastic crowds. Dickens died of exhaustion and a stroke in his own home at the age of 58. He is buried in Poet's Corner in Westminster Abbey.

Historical and social context

Time and place

Although Dickens wrote *Great Expectations* in 1860 and 1861, when he was 48, the action of the novel takes place in the early part of the 19th century, between about 1810 and 1840. Dickens clearly locates the action in this time period by referring to specific London landmarks, such old London Bridge (which was demolished and replaced in 1831) and to the fact that all the journeys in the novel are made either on foot or in coaches or boats, therefore before the use of railway.

The story is set in Kent and London, the two places where Dickens grew up and which he knew well, both from his boyhood and throughout his life as a writer. Dickens had homes in various different parts of London as well as at Gad's Hill outside Rochester where *Great Expectations* was partly set (though not specifically identified as such in the book). Dickens's familiarity with both the setting and the period helps to give the novel a very solid sense of time and place.

In choosing to set the action in contrasting locations, Dickens is able to highlight the differences between the relative peace and tranquillity of Pip's boyhood village, with its church, tavern and smithy, and where everyone knew everyone else's business, with the crowded, dirty city of London, full of dangers and strangers that Pip discovers when he arrives in 'Little Britain'. The reality of London offers a sharp contrast to Pip's anticipation of his future life 'so unknown and great' *(Volume 1, Chapter 19)*.

Activity 1

All the locations that Pip refers to in London are real places. Try finding them on a street map of London or on a map of 19th–century London on the Internet.

Much of Victorian London was overcrowded and dirty

The London of *Great Expectations* is a London shaped by the Industrial Revolution of the late 18th and early 19th centuries. Pip describes it on his arrival as 'rather ugly, crooked, narrow, and dirty' *(Volume 2, Chapter 20)*. It was certainly a very overcrowded city, as more and more people moved there from the country in search of work. The **Industrial Revolution** also made greater **social mobility** possible.

Industrial Revolution a time when more people began to work in industry rather than agriculture. They left the countryside and moved close to the factories and mills in large cities, from where the manufactured goods were exported

social mobility the ability of members of the lower classes to acquire wealth through their own efforts and 'rise' up the class system, rather than being born into a moneyed background

Social class and social mobility

The plot of *Great Expectations* is based on Pip's change in status from a blacksmith's apprentice to a gentleman of leisure, so it is vitally important to understand the significance of social class in the early 19th century. Although it is conventional to divide society into three broad classes – upper, middle and lower – there are many distinctions even within these categories.

Although a simplification, it is possible to see the class system as a pyramid, with royalty at the top and the working classes near the bottom, just above the homeless and vagrant people.

Royalty

Aristocracy Hereditary peers/
landowners
Baronets the hereditary
version of knights

Upper classes: including those in high
office in Church, law, military, medicine
Knights: created by royalty/government for
services rendered to the monarch or state
Gentry: educated landowners, wealthy
enough not to have to work to earn money

Upper middle class: lower-ranking, university-educated
professionals
Wealthy industrialists employing large numbers
of workers in their factories/mines/mills

Lower middle classes: 'white collar' workers
in clerical and administrative jobs

Working classes, including shop workers and medical
auxiliaries at the higher end

Hundreds of thousands of labourers, in mines, mills,
factories and farms, working very hard for very, very little

The homeless and vagrants, including prostitutes, living
hand-to-mouth and/or begging for food. Some lived in workhouses
rather than starve to death

Others, even lower down the social scale, did starve to death in this period

▲ The social classes in 19th-century England

Nobody from the highest categories of class appears in *Great Expectations*, although Mrs Pocket's father believed **'that his deceased father would have been made a Baronet but for somebody's determined opposition'** *(Volume 2, Chapter 23)* and Mrs Pocket is obsessed with social class and mightily disappointed in her husband for not being an aristocrat. Bentley Drummle represents the nearest thing to an aristocrat in the novel as he is **'next heir but one to a baronetcy'** *(Volume 2, Chapter 23)* but he is plain Mister Drummle, with no title of his own.

Miss Havisham is a lady whose fortune is based on commerce; her father was a successful brewer. Her position as a lady of wealth and property attracted the fortune hunter Compeyson. She is not upper class but upper middle class; she has no need to work for a living because she has property and tenants, including Mr Pumblechook.

Jaggers, a prominent lawyer who works principally defending members of the criminal class, is also upper middle class. Even though he is employed as Miss Havisham's legal adviser, his education and profession make him her equal in terms of class.

Matthew and Herbert Pocket are in the same class, both having to work for a living, but they are **genteel** and Matthew Pocket was educated at Harrow School and Cambridge University.

Genteel Victorian society

aristocracy people whose ancestors received land and/or titles from a king or queen, which have then been passed down through the generations. The titles have their own fine distinctions

baronet an aristocrat ranked below a baron but above a knight, addressed as 'Sir' like a knight

genteel well-mannered and refined

Key facts about Victorian schools and universities

The most prestigious schools (for boys) at the time were Harrow, Eton and Winchester. Cambridge and Oxford Universities are the oldest in England and the only ones that existed at the beginning of the 19th century.

Wemmick is a good example of someone who has improved himself in times of social mobility. The Aged P tells Pip that Wemmick had originally been destined to be a wine-cooper (someone who makes casks or barrels for wine or ale) but that he went into the law to be able to provide a home for the Aged P once he had given up work. Wemmick is therefore lower middle class. This category also covers Pumblechook, a corn-chandler who owns a shop. His ownership of a chaise-cart is further evidence of his wealth and position in the town. Wopsle, the church clerk, is also educated and belongs to this class.

Joe's skilled trade as a blacksmith puts him above the general mass of the working classes. Any trade that required an apprenticeship, such as blacksmith or wheelwright (Mr Hubble), lifted the skilled man above the common class of labourer, as Orlick becomes.

Lower-class characters include all unskilled workers, servants and maids and, in London, gate-keepers and porters. Below this, Magwitch and Molly (before she was rescued by Jaggers) fall into the vagrant class, including petty criminals and homeless people.

Key quotations

"What is your real name?" I asked him in a whisper.

"Magwitch," he answered, in the same tone; "chrisen'd Abel."

"What were you brought up to be?"

"A warmint, dear boy."

He answered quite seriously, and used the word as if it denoted some profession. *(Volume 3, Chapter 40)*

Activity 2

1. In pairs, consider how much these classifications relate to the situation people are born into and how much they depend on hard work.

2. Where would you place Estella in this **hierarchy** and why?

hierarchy a system of ranking, from the most superior to the most inferior

Education

There was no such thing as state-funded, compulsory education in Dickens's lifetime. Boys from upper-class families were sent to private schools such as Winchester, Eton or Harrow, at considerable expense, or they were privately tutored by scholars like Matthew Pocket. The children of the middle classes attended local grammar schools or cathedral schools, which existed in most cities, where fees were more modest.

Children from working-class families were least likely to go to school. Those who did often learned how to read and write (but little more than this) at Sunday School or by paying two pence a week to attend Dame schools, the kind of evening school run by Mr Wopsle's great aunt. However, in the wake of the Industrial Revolution, thousands of children worked long hours, all week, in factories, mills or agricultural labouring jobs, and received no education of any kind. Their parents lived in too much poverty to manage without their children's wages, let alone to pay a few pence a week for them to go to school.

Although there was much talk in Parliament in the early 1800s about the desirability of ensuring that all children received some form of education, it was actually argued by a great many respectable and influential figures that educating the masses would be dangerous for society as a whole, as it would make working-class children dissatisfied with the menial work they were 'born' to do.

Many children in Victorian England had to work in factories and had little or no time for education

Activity 3

In pairs, try to find as many references to education, learning and improvement as you can in the novel. As a starting place you might re-read Chapters 7, 15 and 24 in Volume 1 and Chapter 42 in Volume 3, and think about the education received by Joe, Pip, Estella, Biddy and Magwitch.

Crime, punishment and prison

From the very beginning of the book, Pip is made aware of convicts, of prison ships (the Hulks), crime and punishment. Within hours of arriving in London, he has been given a tour of Newgate prison, seen the door condemned men and women pass through to be executed and seen the gallows that they were hanged from, in public, and for the entertainment of onlookers. Later, Wemmick gives Pip a more intimate tour of the prison when he goes to talk to some of Jaggers' clients.

The British criminal justice system in the early part of the 19th century was very harsh. Theft of petty items such as a bag of onions might result in the thief spending many years in prison, often in solitary confinement with a period of **hard labour** to follow.

Crime was on the increase as cities became overcrowded and, when factories laid off their workers when trade was bad, some had little alternative but to turn to crime. This put pressure on the existing prisons, which was why at the end of the 18th century the authorities started to transport some criminals to Australia, where Britain was establishing a colony. Even stealing small sums of money or an animal resulted in the death penalty. It was one way to empty overcrowded prisons.

Dickens shows, through his presentation of the unequal treatment of Compeyson and Magwitch, how unfair the criminal justice system in the early 19th century was. Because Compeyson had been to public school, was a smooth talker and had the appearance of a gentleman, the law was more lenient with him than it was with Magwitch, who the courts viewed as a hardened criminal, despite the fact that Compeyson was the brains behind the forgery scam that landed them both in court.

We are also shown that even lawyers like Jaggers resort to dishonest methods, manipulating the justice system as seen in Volume 2, Chapter 20 where one of his potential witnesses, willing to swear to 'anythink' turns out to be 'a murderous-looking tall individual' with a black eye, dressed up as a 'sort of pastry-cook' *(Volume 2, Chapter 20)*. Although Jaggers dismisses him as being preposterous, it is evident that he has used more plausible-looking false witnesses before in defence of his clients.

What chance does ignorant, poor Magwitch have in the face of such 'justice'?

> **Key quotations**
>
> "This is the way it was, that when I was a ragged little creetur as much to be pitied as ever I see… I got the name of being hardened. 'This is a terrible hardened one,' they says to prison wisitors, picking out me. 'May be said to live in jails, this boy.'… They always went on agen me about the Devil. But what the Devil was I to do? I must put something into my stomach, mustn't I?" *(Volume 3, Chapter 42)*

Activity 4

Find out all you can about the prison system that resulted in Magwitch being sent to Australia. There is plenty of information on the Internet, including an excellent website called 'Victorian Crime and Punishment'.

Christian teaching

Great Expectations was written at a time when Britain was a largely Christian society and where regular attendance at church was part of family life. Even those who could not read and write would have been familiar with the Bible through listening to sermons and readings at church services.

Although *Great Expectations* is not explicitly about religion, it does have strong overtones of Christian teaching. Pip's 'journey' towards more fully understanding himself can be compared in some ways to the journey of the character Christian in Bunyan's Christian **allegory**, *A Pilgrim's Progress*. Both Pip and Christian spend much of their 'journey' loaded with guilt about their 'sins' and encounter a range of extraordinary good and bad characters along the way.

> **allegory** a piece of literature which carries a spiritual, moral or political meaning and in which characters and/or events are clearly symbolic of something else
>
> **hard labour** the back-breaking work many prisoners were sentenced to carry out, such as breaking rocks in a quarry, building roads or labouring on the docks. Some prisoners had to walk a treadmill all day with no end product but exhaustion
>
> **penitent** showing or feeling sorrow for wrongdoing

There are further allusions to Christian teaching throughout the novel. Volume 1, Chapter 1 is set in a churchyard on Christmas Eve and Pip's excuse for being late home on Christmas Day is that he has been out listening to the carols. When Pip goes to church with Joe on Christmas Day he feels in need of confession and the conversation around the Christmas dinner table turns to sermons and swine (pigs), 'the companions of the prodigal' *(Volume 1, Chapter 4)*.

> ### Key facts about 'The Prodigal Son'
>
> The parable of 'The Prodigal Son', found in St Luke's Gospel in the Bible, is especially relevant to Pip, who, like the prodigal, leaves his home, squanders his money and finally returns to beg and receive forgiveness from his father figure, Joe.

The Christian virtue of forgiveness is frequently sought, with Miss Havisham finally begging for forgiveness from Pip; Pip begging forgiveness from Joe and Biddy; and Pip praying to God for his forgiveness of Magwitch and to be merciful to him, "a sinner" *(Volume 3, Chapter 56)*. Also, when Pip is recovering from his long illness and discovers that Joe has been caring for him throughout, he whispers, **penitently**, "O God bless him! O God bless this gentle Christian man!" *(Volume 3, Chapter 57)*

These are not the only occasions where conventional Christian ideas are used. There are references to angels and devils, to blessings and curses throughout, and Joe is consistently remembered by the older Pip as full of Christian qualities. In Volume 1, Chapter 18, after Jaggers has revealed Pip's 'great expectations' to him, Pip associates Joe with an angel.

Literary context

Dickens had been a successful novelist for over 20 years when he wrote *Great Expectations* and it could be said that his literary context was partly created by himself, although some of his contemporaries included the authors George Eliot, the Brontës, Thackeray and his great friend, Wilkie Collins, to name but a few. Dickens had already written another novel in the first person, *David Copperfield*, published ten years before *Great Expectations*. This was a semi-autobiographical work exploring aspects of his own childhood and early manhood, and it had been a huge success.

One of Dickens's big influences was the theatre and, at the time he was writing, there was a taste for mysteries and melodramas as well as more classical drama.

Bildungsroman

A Bildungsroman is a novel that traces the development of a character from childhood to adulthood and is often presented as a quest for identity. The leading character matures and gains an insight into his or her own nature as well as into the society that helps to shape their character. Other names for Bildungsroman include education novel, formation novel or coming-of-age novel.

The first Bildungsroman was Goethe's novel *Wilhelm Meister's Apprenticeship*, published in Germany in 1795. Other examples of the genre include Charlotte Brontë's *Jane Eyre* and Mark Twain's *Huckleberry Finn*, as well as Dickens's own *David Copperfield*. The aim was to entertain as well as enlighten the reader.

The Gothic novel

The Gothic novel, sometimes referred to as 'Gothic horror' is a type of literature that combines horror with romance. The English author Horace Walpole is credited with 'inventing' the **genre** with his 1764 novel *The Castle of Otranto*.

Typical 'ingredients' of the Gothic novel include mysterious events, ghosts, madness, secrets and perversions. The plot is often set in a castle, ruin, mansion or haunted house, with villains, madmen, monks, ghosts, magicians and even vampires or werewolves, as in Bram Stoker's *Dracula*. The aim is to thrill and horrify the reader.

genre a literary category such as comedy, tragedy, romance

Sensation fiction

Sensation fiction was an offshoot of the Gothic novel and achieved popularity in the 1860s. The best-known novels in this genre are probably Wilkie Collins's *The Woman in White* and Mary Braddon's *Lady Audley's Secret*. The form was named 'sensation fiction' because it drew on a popular genre of contemporary drama named 'sensation drama'. The plots were less likely than Gothic literature to deal with mysteries and more likely to deal with scandals, crimes and domestic violence. The aim was to shock or scandalize the reader.

There are some elements of the Gothic literary tradition in *Great Expectations*, especially in the setting of Satis House, a symbol of ruin and decay, with its winding corridors, dark passages and abandoned brewery. Similarly, there are some elements that would be familiar to readers of Wilkie Collins' sensation novels, especially in the unfolding mystery of Estella's parentage and her murderess mother Molly.

The Gothic elements in *Dracula*, and stories like it, thrilled and horrified the Victorians

The fierce figure of Magwitch is also quite a 'sensational' character. However, if we try to categorize the novel beyond the general term 'Bildungsroman', it would be reasonable to say that the novel is most clearly categorized as 'Dickensian' – a big novel with a good story at its centre, plenty of humour, plenty of suspense, peopled with a host of characters, some comical, some less so, some low-living and some gentlefolk, and dominated by a hero who, for all his faults, is difficult not to like.

Activity 5

a) Use the Internet to find definitions of 'comedy', 'tragedy' and 'romance' genres.

b) In groups, see whether there are aspects of Dickens's novel that match the genres of Gothic, sensation fiction, comedy, tragedy and romance.

Writing about context

Upgrade

While knowing the social and historical context of the novel will help you to understand the themes of the text more clearly, be wary of introducing background material not strictly relevant to the questions. It will be helpful as you read *Great Expectations* to have given some thought to early 19th-century attitudes towards:

- class and social mobility
- crime, prisons and punishment
- children and their education
- Christian teachings about charity and forgiveness.

Refer to these in your answers where questions ask you about context.

Main characters

Pip is the most important character as it is his experiences and thoughts that make up the substance of the book. Other key figures can be seen to complement or contrast with one another as significant characters in Pip's life.

Activity 1

Before reading on, try to name as many characters (major and minor) as you can remember and put them into groups. Think about who we meet in different volumes. Work in pairs.

Pip

It's important to remember that, because Pip is the narrator as well as the main character, Dickens presents his character both through what Pip tells us directly and what he reports himself as saying and doing. All the other characters are presented as filtered through Pip's eyes. However, Pip is not an **omniscient** narrator and can only 'guess' about what other characters may mean by what they say and do. He is narrating events in his life from the **perspective** of a man in his mid-thirties but principally writing about himself between the ages of seven and twenty-three.

Pip and Herbert, the 'pale young gentleman', meet each other as boys (*Great Expectations*, 2012)

For example, in Volume 1, Chapter 2, Pip writes about what his sister does to him when she suspects him of 'bolting' his bread and butter. His language is simple and perfectly catches the sense of a little boy's memory: **'My sister made a dive at me, and fished me up by the hair, saying nothing more than the awful words, "You come along and be dosed"'** (*Volume 1, Chapter 2*).

Later in the same chapter we hear the distinctly adult voice of Pip expressing the terrors of a young boy but using the sophisticated language of the mature narrator:

'At other times, I thought, What if the young man who was with so much difficulty restrained from imbruing his hands in me, should yield to a constitutional impatience, or should mistake the time, and should think himself accredited to my heart and liver to-night, instead of to-morrow! If ever anybody's hair stood on end with terror, mine must have done so then. But, perhaps, nobody's ever did?' *(Volume 1, Chapter 2)*

Tips for assessment

When you are looking at extracts from the novel in your assessments, you should pay close attention to the narrative voice and how it changes from simple and childlike to more complicated and sophisticated depending upon which Pip – the boy or the man – is telling the story.

Activity 2

a) Look for further examples of where Pip, the narrator, switches from the perspective of his youthful self to the perspective of the older, wiser writer. The early chapters of Volume 1 provide many examples.

b) In each case look at how Dickens chooses more complex vocabulary and sentence structures to reflect the older viewpoint.

Great Expectations is about Pip's journey from childhood to adulthood and his quest to discover his own place in the world. His character changes as he matures.

At the beginning of the novel Pip is an innocent child who suffers at the rough hands of his sister Mrs Joe, while enjoying the company and protection of Joe.

Pip is initially both innocent and kind. His act of providing Magwitch with food and brandy is prompted by fear but he also shows sympathy towards him. He is concerned about his symptoms of the **ague**, takes pleasure in seeing Magwitch enjoy his food and brandy, and shows compassion for the convicts the soldiers are hunting, whispering, **"I hope, Joe, we shan't find them"** *(Volume 1, Chapter 5)*.

> **ague** a fever, much like the 'flu'
>
> **omniscient** knowing everything, as an omniscient narrator does about the characters, including their inner thoughts and motivations
>
> **perspective** in literature, a point of view; perception of the situation

Once Pip has been to Miss Havisham's, he begins to change. Estella's comments about his **"thick boots"** and **"coarse hands"** *(Volume 1, Chapter 8)* wound Pip and he walks home feeling **'that I was much more ignorant than I had considered myself last night, and generally that I was in a low-lived bad way'** *(Volume 1, Chapter 8)*. From this point, Pip begins to judge his own home life and sees it as 'common'. Unable to put his real experiences at Satis House into words, he invents elaborate lies about the games that he played with Miss Havisham and Estella. Feeling guilty about deceiving Joe (but not his sister or Pumblechook), he confesses to Joe that he made up the story about the flags, the dogs and the veal cutlets and, despite Joe's encouraging words about Pip being **"oncommon"** *(Volume 1, Chapter 9)*, he believes Estella's judgement of him.

In the next stage, his infatuation with Estella grows and he develops an ambition to become a gentleman, although his understanding of the term 'gentleman' is very narrow. He becomes embarrassed by Joe's appearance and behaviour at Satis House and, on being apprenticed to Joe, he feels miserable.

Key facts about the status of a 'gentleman'

There are several different definitions of what a 'gentleman' is. Historically, from the medieval era to the early 18th century, the term 'gentleman' applied to someone who was not of noble birth, but whose family had a **coat of arms**. A gentleman ranked above a yeoman, a 'commoner' who owned and cultivated their own land.

The definition that Pip seems to have in mind is that of an educated man of higher social class than his own, with an independent income.

The broader definition of the term, and one that allows characters as different as Joe Gargery and Matthew Pocket to deserve the name of 'gentleman', is someone who treats others with courtesy and thoughtfulness.

coat of arms a unique design of symbols and colours, drawn/painted on a shield to represent an individual or family; coats of arms originated in medieval times

Key quotations

I had believed in the forge as the glowing road to manhood and independence. Within a single year, all this was changed. Now it was all coarse and common, and I would not have had Miss Havisham and Estella see it on any account. *(Volume 1, Chapter 14)*

Pip's 'expectations' and his move to London bring further change. He meets new people and proves himself a good friend to both Wemmick and Herbert, whom he helps onto his career path. However, he abandons his old friends Joe and Biddy, and by avoiding seeing them on his frequent visits to Miss Havisham, he shows himself to be ungrateful.

Pip becomes a snob and a **spendthrift**. Leading a lavish lifestyle, he gets into debt.

The older Pip tells us he wasn't happy, despite all his money, and we see that his frequent meetings with Estella bring him only misery.

His life changes again when Magwitch reappears and turns out to be Pip's benefactor. Pip feels no gratitude at first, only revulsion. His decision not to take any more of Magwitch's money could be seen as a noble gesture, but others see it as foolish, even ungrateful. As Pip learns more about Magwitch's terrible life of hardship and imprisonment, he begins to feel affection for the man who has risked his own life to return to him.

In the latter stages of his development, Pip learns to forgive. He forgives Miss Havisham for wilfully deceiving him and he risks his own life, saving her from the fire. He does all he can to help Magwitch get safely out of the country but when the scheme fails, he supports him to the end.

The final stage of Pip's development is after Magwitch's death. Joe's tender nursing of him through his dangerous illness restores Pip's appreciation of the father figure who protected him in his childhood. He recognizes Joe for the "gentle Christian man" (Volume 3, Chapter 57) that he has been throughout his life and is reconciled with him and Biddy before he leaves England to work with Herbert at Clarriker's.

> **spendthrift** someone who spends money freely and without regard to cost

Activity 3

Work in pairs to find evidence of Pip's good qualities as well as his faults.

a) List all Pip's qualities.
b) Find relevant references and quotations to support your list.
c) Comment on what each reference reveals about Pip.

As he is the main character, Pip is associated with all of the themes in the novel. His name suggests a pip or seed that will grow to be a man.

Joe Gargery

Joe is a very significant character, representing honesty, goodness and Christian virtues such as forgiveness and 'turning the other cheek'.

Key facts about the teaching of Jesus

In St Luke's Gospel in the Bible (Chapter 6, Verse 2), Luke reports Jesus's sermon in which he instructs his followers, 'And unto him that smiteth thee on the one cheek offer also the other'. Here, Jesus is using a figure of speech to preach against seeking revenge for a hurt.

In Chapter 7 we hear about Joe's violent father who 'hammered' *(Volume 1, Chapter 7)* both Joe and his mother. This experience taught him that it was wrong for a man to hit a woman and led him to be uncomplaining with his own aggressive wife. He puts up with her ranting and abuse, always adopting a 'conciliatory air' *(Volume 1, Chapter 4)* when she turns on him, despite his great physical strength. He has forgiven his abusive father, puts up with his wife's 'rampages' and is an exemplary father figure to Pip, protecting him as far as he can.

Joe provides Pip and Mrs Joe with a comfortable home. It may not be a manor house like Satis House, and Pip comes to be ashamed of both Joe and his home at the forge, but the family are not poor. In an age where all road transport was horse-drawn, a blacksmith, providing the horseshoes, was a key figure in any community and assured of regular trade.

Although Mrs Joe frequently insults Joe, calling him a "staring great stuck pig" *(Volume 1, Chapter 2)*, "Mooncalf" *(Volume 1, Chapter 7)* and "the dunder-headed king of the noodles" *(Volume 1, Chapter 15)* among other things, he is no fool. In his conversations with Pip and in some of his interactions with his shrewish wife he proves himself to be sensible, moral and perceptive. He handles Mrs Joe's temper with great tact and skill; for example, when Mrs Joe is outraged about being excluded from Joe's invitation to Satis House, Joe delivers an invented, conciliatory message from Miss Havisham to his wife.

Key quotations

"What she giv'," said Joe, "she giv' to his friends." 'And by his friends,' were her explanation, 'I mean into the hands of his sister Mrs. J. Gargery.' Them were her words; 'Mrs. J. Gargery.' She mayn't have know'd," added Joe, with an appearance of reflection, "whether it were Joe, or Jorge." *(Volume 1, Chapter 13)*

When Pip is little, Joe is a constant friend and the two key phrases that he uses to remind Pip of their early comradeship echo through the book, "what larks!" *(Volume 3, Chapter 57)* and "Ever the best of friends" *(Volume 1, Chapter 7)*. Joe teaches Pip to respect himself when he comes back from Satis House, ashamed of being 'common'. He teaches him not to tell lies but he is not angry when Pip does.

Joe is entirely selfless in his dealings with Pip. He refuses to accept money from Jaggers to release Pip from his apprenticeship and only wishes Pip well. He does not take offence at Pip's disgracefully snobbish treatment of him when he visits him at Barnard's Inn.

He never reproaches Pip for not visiting him once he has come into his 'expectations', even after Mrs Joe's funeral, when Joe is left alone.

Activity 4

In pairs, improvise a conversation between Joe and Biddy, discussing Pip once he has left, following his sister's funeral. What do you think they might say about him?

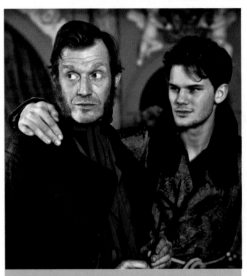

Pip comes to value Joe's good and gentle qualities

When Pip eventually falls ill, it is Joe who nurses him back to health, rekindles the bond of love between them, settles Pip's debts, then withdraws in a dignified manner when he senses that Pip is strong enough to do without him. In this way, he reveals his steadfast loyalty to Pip as well as his forgiveness of Pip's earlier signs of ingratitude. When Pip finally does return to the forge and begs Joe's forgiveness, he gives it willingly, adding, **"if I have anythink to forgive!"** *(Volume 3, Chapter 58).*

Not well-spoken, nor educated, self-conscious in the company of strangers, and looking ridiculous (to Pip) in his best clothes, Joe is nevertheless the true gentleman of the novel. Only the shallow characters in the novel patronize Joe; those with **discrimination**, like Biddy and even Miss Havisham, see the goodness in the man.

Key quotations

Miss Havisham glanced at him as if she understood what he really was better than I had thought possible, seeing what he was there; and took up a little bag from the table beside her.

"Pip has earned a premium here," she said, "and here it is. There are five-and-twenty guineas in this bag. Give it to your master, Pip?" *(Volume 1, Chapter 13)*

conciliatory aimed at keeping the peace
discrimination the ability to make accurate judgements

Dickens has made it almost impossible for readers not to admire Joe, as well as to laugh at some of his expressions. That he is rewarded with Biddy as his wife at the end of the book is the real happy ending.

Activity 5

Look through the chapters that feature Joe and pick out some of his mispronounced words. For example, in Volume 2, Chapter 27 he describes the drawing of the blacking warehouse as **'too architectooralooral'** *(Volume 2, Chapter 27)*. What effects is Dickens intending to achieve with this verbal **idiosyncrasy** of Joe's?

Joe is associated with themes of parenting, education, what it means to be a gentleman and Christian virtues. The name Joseph means 'to increase'. He functions as a model of paternal care.

Mrs Joe

Pip's sister is known as 'Mrs Joe'. She is not given an identity of her own and she is presented, initially, as something of a comical **caricature**.

Key quotations

My sister, Mrs. Joe, with black hair and eyes, had such a prevailing redness of skin that I sometimes used to wonder whether it was possible she washed herself with a nutmeg-grater instead of soap. She was tall and bony, and almost always wore a coarse apron, fastened over her figure behind with two loops, and having a square impregnable bib in front, that was stuck full of pins and needles. *(Volume 1, Chapter 2)*

However, there is little comical about the way she treats her little brother, on whom she seems to vent all her frustrations with her life as a blacksmith's wife, "and him a Gargery" *(Volume 1, Chapter 2)*.

Key quotations

When I reached home, my sister was very curious to know all about Miss Havisham's, and asked a number of questions. And I soon found myself getting heavily bumped from behind in the nape of the neck and the small of the back, and having my face ignominiously shoved against the kitchen wall, because I did not answer those questions at sufficient length. *(Volume 1, Chapter 9)*

This quotation shows the kind of physical force that Mrs Joe employs in her rearing of Pip, 'by hand', and it by no means suggests a sisterly affection for her brother.

Mrs Joe is clearly not happy in her marriage and, despite Joe's view that she is a "fine figure of a woman" *(Volume 1, Chapter 7)*, she has no such words of admiration for him. She is contemptuous of Joe's mild temper, treating him with hostility and aggression. She speaks to Joe and about him as if he were an annoying child.

Activity 6

Can you see any reason why Mrs Joe is so angry all the time? Try to come up with two or three points to explain her frustrations.

Mrs Joe is only ever polite with visitors, like the Hubbles and Mr Wopsle, who make her feel important in her status as hostess, putting on a show of graciousness, especially towards the relatively wealthy Uncle Pumblechook, who flatters her while patronizing Joe, his real nephew.

When Pumblechook is asked to find a boy to play at Miss Havisham's, his recommendation of Pip leads Mrs Joe to think that **"this boy's fortune may be made by his going to Miss Havisham's"** *(Volume 1, Chapter 7)*. She reveals her **mercenary** nature by speculating that Miss Havisham would **"do something"** *(Volume 1, Chapter 9)* for Pip. Given her apparent lack of affection for her brother, Mrs Joe is certainly hoping for advantages for herself, rather than for Pip.

Orlick's violent attack on Mrs Joe leaves her as a permanent invalid, yet her character softens. Now completely helpless, her 'rampaging' days are over. She becomes patient and submissive, and appears to take comfort in Orlick's presence. Before she dies, she shows some remorse for her treatment of both Joe and Pip.

caricature an exaggerated and often comical presentation of a character; presented in words or as a cartoon

idiosyncrasy a recognizable personal habit

mercenary motivated by money

Key quotations

"She made signs to me that she wanted him to sit down close to her, and wanted me to put her arms round his neck. So I put them round his neck, and she laid her head down on his shoulder quite content and satisfied. And so she presently said 'Joe' again, and once 'Pardon,' and once 'Pip.' And so she never lifted her head up any more, and it was just an hour later when we laid it down on her own bed, because we found she was gone." *(Volume 2, Chapter 35)*

It is worth noting that Dickens does not allow the reader any access to Mrs Joe's 'inner life' and we learn nothing of her private feelings or thoughts. Unlike Joe and Magwitch, who Dickens allows to tell something of their own story in direct conversation with Pip, Mrs Joe never confides details about her past life to anyone.

What we do know about her is that, like Pip, she has been orphaned and lost five brothers. We know she took responsibility for rearing her little brother and that her decision to do so was admired in the neighbourhood. We know that when Joe was courting Mrs Joe he made it plain to her that 'the poor little child' *(Volume 1, Chapter 7)* was welcome at the forge when they got married. If Mrs Joe was a real person rather than a character in a novel, we might wonder whether she had sacrificed her own happiness to look after Pip and, possibly, that she only married Joe to provide a stable home for them both.

Activity 7

In pairs, write a conversation between Biddy and Mrs Joe, starting with Biddy asking, 'How did you come to be married to the blacksmith, Mrs Joe?' Imagine the sorts of things that have led to her becoming the dissatisfied wife that Dickens presents.

Mrs Joe is associated with the themes of parenthood, wealth and materialism, forgiveness and redemption. In Volume 3, Chapter 58, Pumblechook reveals that "her name was Georgiana M'ria", but we never hear anyone address her in this way. She functions as a flawed mother figure, a violent character who is finally subdued by violence.

Uncle Pumblechook

Uncle Pumblechook is another of Dickens's caricatures, as indicated by his silly name. Although Pumblechook is not physically violent towards Pip, he is a close ally of Mrs Joe's and consistently torments Pip by lecturing him and bombarding him with mental arithmetic sums, even over breakfast.

Pumblechook introduces Pip to Miss Havisham and, like Mrs Joe, he expects that Miss Havisham will reward Pip. Pumblechook suggests this reward might be a 'handsome premium' for Pip to be bound apprentice to some 'genteel trade' *(Volume 1, Chapter 9)* such as his own, revealing his hopes to benefit personally from that money.

Pumblechook takes Pip to Satis House

Once Pip receives his mysterious 'expectations', Pumblechook takes all the credit and continues to boast of his role in Pip's fortunes long after Pip has gone to London.

Pumblechook is one of the few characters that the mature Pip looks back upon with unmixed feelings of hostility.

> **Key quotations**
>
> ... Uncle Pumblechook, a large hard-breathing middle-aged slow man, with a mouth like a fish, dull staring eyes, and sandy hair standing upright on his head, so that he looked as if he had just been all but choked, and had that moment come to... *(Volume 1, Chapter 4)*
>
> That ass, Pumblechook, used often to come over of a night for the purpose of discussing my prospects with my sister... *(Volume 1, Chapter 12)*
>
> "It's five-and-twenty pound, Mum," echoed that basest of swindlers, Pumblechook... *(Volume 1, Chapter 13)*

Because of the consistently negative presentation of Pumblechook and his own pompous and insufferable behaviour, there is some satisfaction for the reader when Joe describes how Pumblechook's shop was burgled and his uncle was humiliated.

> **Key quotations**
>
> "... they took his till, and they took his cash-box, and they drinked his wine, and they partook of his wittles, and they slapped his face, and they pulled his nose, and they tied him up to his bedpust, and they giv' him a dozen, and they stuffed his mouth full of flowering annuals to prewent his crying out." *(Volume 3, Chapter 57)*

Activity 8

Re-read Volume 1, Chapter 19, then answer the following questions.

a) Why do you think Dickens makes Pumblechook's behaviour towards Pip so different here? Compare the meal that Pip enjoys here with the Christmas lunch at the forge in Volume 1, Chapter 4.

b) Why do you think Pip's opinion of Pumblechook is different here?

Pumblechook is linked to the themes of children, class and identity. His name, which blends a word close to 'bumble' with the word 'chook', which means 'hen or chicken', suggests both his bumbling interference and clucking nature, helping to create his comical presentation. He functions as a foil to Joe and a representative of a society motivated by greed and self-interest.

Miss Havisham

Miss Havisham is not one of Dickens's caricatures as there is little that is comical in her presentation, but she is an exaggerated rather than a realistic character and much of the detail about her is **implausible**. She is an intentionally mysterious figure whose background and circumstances are unravelled for the reader bit by bit as Pip grows older and acquires more information about her.

As a character, Miss Havisham is defined by the fact that she was **jilted** on her wedding day. As a result of this humiliation, she attempted to stop time – which can never be done. However, all the clocks and watches in Satis House have been stopped at **'twenty minutes to nine'** *(Volume 1, Chapter 8)*, the moment when she discovered her wedding was 'off'. Miss Havisham appears to have suffered some sort of breakdown as a result of her experience. She is obstinately indifferent to hours, days and weeks, and has plunged her home into perpetual darkness, blocking up the windows from the daylight so that she does not have to count the passage of time.

When Pip first sees her, Miss Havisham is portrayed as having worn her wedding dress, veil and wedding shoes constantly over many years. Her bridal feast, crowned by a great wedding cake, stands rotting in the room across the hall from her dressing room. Miss Havisham has therefore sacrificed herself and all possibilities of a happy, normal existence as a curse on the man who ruined her life by abandoning her on her wedding day.

> **implausible** far-fetched; creative yet improbable; for example, wearing the same dress for 20 years without it falling in rags
>
> **jilted** abandoned, usually on a wedding day

Activity 9

What other aspects of Miss Havisham's life appear implausible? In small groups, make a list of these.

As the novel progresses, we learn that Miss Havisham's lover was Compeyson, the so-called 'gentleman', whose outward appearance misled Miss Havisham to accept him as a suitable husband but whose motives in wooing her were entirely mercenary. Dickens presents Miss Havisham's situation symbolically, comparing how she was abandoned by Compeyson with the way she abandons her life, her house, her father's brewery and any meaningful contact with the outside world. Miss Havisham re-invents herself as a living symbol of what it means to be heartbroken.

Through Jaggers, her lawyer and only link with the outside world, she finds a little girl to adopt and to inflict revenge on the male sex. Miss Havisham tells Pip that her first motive was only **"to save her from misery"** but that gradually **"I stole her heart away, and put ice in its place"** *(Volume 3, Chapter 49)*.

As a mother figure to Pip she is a complete failure, doing no more for him as a boy than providing a meal on the days he visits her. She appears to enjoy watching him having his heart broken by Estella. In fact, the 25 guineas she gives Joe as Pip's 'premium' is not a fantastic sum, given the hours that Pip has devoted to her whims.

> **Key quotations**
>
> "You can break his heart." *(Volume 1, Chapter 8)*
>
> "Love her, love her, love her! If she favours you, love her. If she wounds you, love her. If she tears your heart to pieces—and as it gets older and stronger, it will tear deeper—love her, love her, love her!" *(Volume 2, Chapter 29)*

Miss Havisham finally understands the pain and misery she has caused

Miss Havisham finally sees the consequences of her actions, realizing, too late, how unnatural a young woman she has made Estella and that Estella's life will be miserable with Bentley Drummle. She also suddenly sees, looking at Pip as if in a "looking-glass" *(Volume 3, Chapter 49)*, that she has caused him the same heartbreak that she suffered and that he has done nothing to deserve it.

> **Key quotations**
>
> "My name is on the first leaf. If you can ever write under my name, 'I forgive her,' though ever so long after my broken heart is dust—pray do it!" *(Volume 3, Chapter 49)*

Although Pip does not fulfil his ambition 'to restore the desolate house, admit the sunshine into the dark rooms, set the clocks a-going and the cold hearths a-blazing, tear down the cobwebs, destroy the vermin' *(Volume 2, Chapter 29)*, he does succeed in bringing Miss Havisham to realize the enormity of the damage she has done to two innocent children. Pip's essential goodness (which, as narrator, he rarely discusses) finally touches Miss Havisham. Her need for Pip's forgiveness, which he readily gives, reveals her remorse, which is seen in her readiness to help Herbert and her final legacy to Matthew Pocket.

Of course, Miss Havisham's main function in the novel is to be the person that Pip believes to be his benefactor. This belief, which Miss Havisham encourages, leads Pip to abandon Joe, setting his sights on marrying the heartless Estella. Pip confronts Miss Havisham once he has discovered the truth.

Key quotations

"In humouring my mistake, Miss Havisham, you punished—practised on—perhaps you will supply whatever term expresses your intention, without offence—your self-seeking relations?" *(Volume 3, Chapter 44)*

Miss Havisham's image is forever haunting Pip's dreams, as well as his waking hours, and his illusions about her blind him to the series of events that point, in quite another direction, to the true identity of his benefactor. In this way, Miss Havisham acts as a smokescreen to the deepest mystery of the book.

Key quotations

…I turned my head to look back… and I fancied that I saw Miss Havisham hanging to the beam. So strong was the impression, that I stood under the beam shuddering from head to foot before I knew it was a fancy—though to be sure I was there in an instant. *(Volume 3, Chapter 49)*

Activity 10

Pip has a vivid imagination and the novel contains many references to 'fancies' like the one in the quotation above, as well as to his dreams and nightmares. In small groups, find as many of these 'sensational' occurrences as you can. List them, then discuss what you think Dickens intended them to contribute to the novel.

Miss Havisham is associated with the themes of identity, class, love and parents. Her name, combining 'have' (possibly meaning 'having' wealth) and 'sham', suggests falsehood. She functions as a flawed mother figure to both Pip and Estella.

Estella

When Pip first meets Estella, she is haughty, proud and cold, and so she remains until the final chapter. She is rude to him and about him, calling him a "common labouring-boy" *(Volume 1, Chapter 8)*. She taunts him and enjoys seeing him cry; she puts his food on the ground, treating him with no more respect than a dog.

During later visits, she slaps him and laughs at him. When Joe is brought with Pip's indentures, Estella's eyes 'laughed mischievously' in mockery of Pip's 'master' *(Volume 1, Chapter 13)*. In return for all her cruelty towards him, Pip adores Estella, believing her to be his guiding 'star'.

After attending 'finishing school' in Paris, Estella is even more attractive to Pip, who continues to worship her despite her many warnings that she has **"no heart"** *(Volume 2, Chapter 29)*. She is honest with Pip, explaining that she does not attempt to **"deceive and entrap"** him *(Volume 2, Chapter 38)*, though she confesses that, following Miss Havisham's intentions for her, she does flirt with other men to entice them.

In fact, Dickens presents both Estella and Pip as victims of Compeyson's cruelty towards Miss Havisham. Estella has been reared **"to wreak revenge on all the male sex"** *(Volume 2, Chapter 22)*, as Herbert explains to Pip. She is therefore destined to live without love – a terrible fate to inflict on an innocent child.

Before Estella marries Bentley Drummle, she and Miss Havisham have the only argument that Pip is ever witness to, when Estella accuses her adoptive mother of making her what she has become.

> **Key quotations**
>
> **"I am what you have made me. Take all the praise, take all the blame; take all the success, take all the failure; in short, take me."** *(Volume 2, Chapter 38)*

She marries Bentley Drummle in spite of Miss Havisham's objections and in spite of Pip's sincere wish that she should marry any other more worthy suitor. Her marriage is unhappy and Drummle is reported to have treated her with **'great cruelty'** *(Volume 3, Chapter 59)*.

Activity 11

Why do you think Estella marries Bentley Drummle?

In Dickens's original ending, Estella and Pip meet by chance in Piccadilly. Estella has remarried after the death of Drummle and sees Pip from her carriage window. They look **'sadly enough on one another'** and shake hands. The final paragraph concludes that **'suffering had been stronger than Miss Havisham's teaching, and had given her a heart to understand what my heart used to be'** *(Volume 3, Chapter 59)*.

Dickens was persuaded to change the ending of the novel to bring about a reunion between Estella and Pip. The changed version is still somewhat ambiguous about their future, but allows the romantics amongst the novel's readers to see something of a 'happy ever after' conclusion.

> I took her hand in mine, and we went out of the ruined place; and, as the morning mists had risen long ago when I first left the forge, so the evening mists were rising now, and in all the broad expanse of tranquil light they showed to me, I saw the shadow of no parting from her. *(Volume 3, Chapter 59)*

Beautiful and elegant in all things, Estella is kept in ignorance of her true parents, Molly and Magwitch. There is great irony in her shrinking from the wretches in Newgate prison and in her snobbish attitude towards common people, when her own parents were from the lowest class of all in society, criminals and vagrants.

Activity 12

Read Dickens's original final chapter, which is available on the Internet as well as being included in many printed editions of the novel. Which version of the ending do you prefer and why?

Estella is associated with the themes of parents and children, identity, social class, love and money. Her name means 'star'. She functions as an unobtainable dream to Pip and as a **foil** to Biddy.

Biddy

Biddy is one of Dickens's most realistic characters. She is an orphan, like Pip, and is presented as a foil to Estella.

Initially, Biddy is Pip's teacher, as she helps to run the Dame school that he attends. Once Pip becomes dissatisfied with himself, as a result of Estella's scorn, it is Biddy he turns to, imploring her to 'impart all her learning' *(Volume 1, Chapter 10)* to him, a task that she immediately begins.

In many ways, Biddy acts as Pip's conscience. She discourages his childish wish to become a 'gentleman', gives him good advice about his motives to spite or to gain Estella, and is a consistent supporter of Joe, who she values at his true worth.

Pip takes Biddy's friendship for granted and appears unaware of her feelings for him. Before Jaggers arrives with the news of Pip's 'great expectations', there are times when Pip considers his future as a partner with Joe and keeping 'company with Biddy' *(Volume 1, Chapter 17)* with a view to marriage. He recognizes Biddy's constancy and even that 'Biddy was immeasurably better than Estella' *(Volume 1, Chapter 17)*, but those thoughts count for nothing once his dream of being a gentleman becomes a reality.

Dickens is very skilful in revealing Biddy's inner life, as he describes some of her actions when she is listening to Pip talk snobbishly about Joe's manners. First, she plucks 'a black currant leaf', then she looks 'closely at the leaf in her hand', then as she becomes more offended, on Joe's behalf, by Pip's obvious snobbery, we are told, 'Biddy, having rubbed the leaf to pieces between her hands... said, "Have you never considered that he may be proud?' *(Volume 1, Chapter 19)*. In this way, Biddy's inner agitation is revealed through her destruction of the leaf.

Biddy helps the reader to see Joe's worth by consistently pointing it out to Pip, both face-to-face and in the letter she sends to tell Pip about Joe's visit, which she concludes with the comment, 'I hope and do not doubt it will be agreeable to see him even though a gentleman, for you had ever a good heart and he is a worthy worthy man' *(Volume 2, Chapter 27)*.

Biddy's marriage to Joe brings together two good and worthy characters. Their fitness as parents to the next little Pip has been demonstrated through all their words and actions in the novel.

Biddy's name (a version of Bridget) means 'exalted one'. She is associated with the themes of childhood and parents, education and improvement, and love. She functions as a voice of common sense.

> ### Activity 13
>
> Biddy seems to get over her initial tender feelings for Pip and she marries Joe. Imagine you are Biddy. Write some diary entries that show her feelings for Pip changing over the years that he is in London.

Jaggers

Jaggers is hired by Magwitch to be Pip's legal guardian until he comes of age, and he makes it plain to Pip that he is paid for his services. Dickens presents Jaggers as a very clever lawyer, "Deep... as Australia" *(Volume 2, Chapter 24)*.

Jaggers is more of a **plot device** than a fully rounded character. His role as Miss Havisham's lawyer brings him to Satis House, where Pip sees him briefly. When he reappears at the Three Jolly Bargeman, Pip jumps to the conclusion that the source of his 'expectations' must be Miss Havisham. Dickens exploits the 'coincidences' that Jaggers defended Molly, rescued Estella from a miserable existence and brought her to Miss Havisham, and that Magwitch is also his client.

> **foil** a contrast to something else
>
> **plot device** a character or an incident in a novel or play whose function is to make the plot work or to make themes more prominent to the reader

Jaggers' inner life is not explored at all. He is distinctively presented through his outward appearance. His signature habits include biting the side of his forefinger, flourishing his pocket handkerchief as a method of intimidating others, and an almost ritualistic washing of his hands with scented soap. His association with the criminal classes appears as an unpleasant necessity in his line of work, which he is keen to scrub away.

Jaggers' interaction with others is generally aggressive. He bullies his clients; we see him try to bully Joe. He has a formal, professional relationship with Wemmick and displays a masterful dominance over his housekeeper Molly.

Jaggers is meant to be a formidable character; Pip is respectful but wary of him. He performs his duties as Pip's guardian in an impersonal way and, although he is surprised by Pip's disclosure that Magwitch is Estella's father, he is careful not to show it.

Jaggers' name suggests a sharp, jagged and dangerous personality. He is associated with the themes of identity, parents and children, crime and punishment, and the law. His function is to be the impartial communicator of Pip's 'expectations' and to complete some of the pieces of the puzzle surrounding Estella.

> **Key quotations**
>
> "Always seems to me," said Wemmick, "as if he had set a mantrap and was watching it. Suddenly—click—you're caught!" *(Volume 2, Chapter 24)*

Activity 14

What is the significance of Jaggers' association with traps in the novel?

Wemmick

Wemmick is one of Dickens's caricatures. Rather than scrubbing the Newgate germs off his hands, as Jaggers does, Wemmick leads a double life and always keeps the office and the castle separate.

In the office, although he is pleasant enough to Pip, Wemmick only expresses official sentiments; at Walworth, where he lives with his Aged P, he is able to speak his mind.

Unlike Jaggers, Wemmick becomes Pip's friend, adviser and a source of sincere friendship. He invites Pip home and helps him arrange Herbert's start with Clarriker. He advises Pip how to keep Magwitch safe. He demonstrates his personal friendship by making sure Pip attends his wedding.

Wemmick and Jaggers in a production at the Vaudeville Theatre, London, 2013

Wemmick's relationship with his Aged P, his affection for Miss Skiffins and his implausible little house make him a hugely likeable character. His obsession with 'portable property' and material wealth contrast with his otherwise wholly positive character.

> ### Activity 15
>
> Why do you think Dickens makes Wemmick so concerned about having 'portable property'? Think about his line of work as well as his 'dependents' – the Aged P and Miss Skiffins.

Wemmick's name is fairly neutral as he is not one of Dickens's ridiculous figures, despite being described initially as a **'dry man'** with a **'square wooden face, whose expression seemed to have been imperfectly chipped out with a dull-edged chisel'** *(Volume 2, Chapter 21).* His 'dry' exterior turns out simply to be part of his office persona. He is associated with the themes of identity, children and parents, crime and punishment, wealth and its acquisition. He functions as a friend and adviser to Pip, and as an emblem of goodness in the dangerous city of London.

Magwitch

Magwitch's miserable personal history is not told until late in the novel when he recounts it to Pip and Herbert. Orphaned and abandoned, Magwitch is a victim in a society with no welfare system and where to be poor and homeless led inevitably to crime. He has to steal to survive and spent his youth **"in jail and out of jail"** *(Volume 3, Chapter 42).* His criminal association with Compeyson and subsequent prison sentence brought him to the 'Hulks' and to the marshes where Pip first meets him trying to escape from yet another jail.

This meeting leaves a lasting impression on both of them, but while Pip shudders at the memory of the encounter with this **'fearful man'** *(Volume 1, Chapter 1),* Magwitch is full of gratitude to the boy who he believes **"kep life"** in him *(Volume 2, Chapter 39).* All the time he is in Australia, Magwitch is plotting and working for 'his' boy, Pip.

Pip's horror when he learns that Magwitch is his sole benefactor does not destroy Magwitch's triumph in seeing Pip's success as a gentleman. He considers himself to be Pip's **'second father'** *(Volume 2, Chapter 39)* and, as we learn later, he finds in Pip a substitute for his little girl, who he loved and believes to be dead.

Dickens presents Magwitch in such a way that the reader sees the humanity in him where Pip does not. As a young boy, Pip is terrified of him and, in his newly acquired role as a 'gentleman', he is revolted by Magwitch's coarseness. By the end of the novel, Pip comes to recognize the essential goodness in Magwitch and he repays his loyalty by staying with him to the end.

Activity 16

What comedy do you find in Dickens's portrayal of Magwitch? Look especially at the way he speaks and at his rough manner of behaving. Discuss this in pairs and gather evidence to support your findings.

Key quotations

"I've been done everything to, pretty well—except hanged. I've been locked up, as much as a silver tea-kittle. I've been carted here and carted there, and put out of this town, and put out of that town, and stuck in the stocks, and whipped and worried and drove."
(Volume 3, Chapter 42)

"Tramping, begging, thieving, working sometimes when I could – though that warn't as often as you may think, till you put the question whether you would ha' been over ready to give me work yourselves—a bit of a poacher, a bit of a labourer, a bit of a wagoner, a bit of a haymaker, a bit of a hawker, a bit of most things that don't pay and lead to trouble, I got to be a man." *(Volume 3, Chapter 42)*

Magwitch's full name is Abel Magwitch. In the Bible, Abel was murdered by his brother Cain in what was described as the first ever murder. Dickens seems to have wanted us to see him as a victim rather than as a villain.

Magwitch is associated with the themes of crime and punishment, parents and children, social class, identity and what it means to be a gentleman. One of his functions is to show what might have happened to Pip, an orphan like Magwitch, if he had not had his sister and Joe.

Herbert Pocket

Pip first knows Herbert as the 'pale young gentleman' *(Volume 1, Chapter 11)* who challenged him to a fight on his second visit to Miss Havisham's. When Pip moves

Pip and Herbert become the best of friends, while getting used to rather an extravagant lifestyle (*Great Expectations*, 2012)

to London he finds that this same young gentleman is to be his first 'flatmate' and subsequently his best friend and confidant.

Herbert is a gentleman, though without the money to live without working. He is optimistic, kindly and thoroughly good. Pip values his friendship and tells him about his love for Estella. Herbert and Pip agree not to discuss the identity of Pip's benefactor, although there is an unspoken understanding that it is Miss Havisham. When the truth is revealed, Herbert stands by Pip and hatches the plan for getting Magwitch abroad.

Activity 17

Make a list of all Herbert's good qualities. Does he have any faults?

Herbert is the son of Matthew Pocket, Pip's tutor, and the ridiculous Mrs Pocket, whose children are not growing but **'tumbling up'** *(Volume 2, Chapter 22)*. Mrs Pocket is obsessed with rank and aristocracy, causing Herbert's delight to be marrying a girl with no fortune and no family, once her father, whom Herbert refers to as **"Gruffandgrim"** *(Volume 3, Chapter 46)*, has died.

Pip has already invested in Herbert's future by secretly buying him a partnership with the young shipping insurer, Clarriker. Pip considers this to be the one good thing he has done with his 'expectations'.

Herbert, whose name means 'bright army', is associated with the themes of love and loyalty, children and parents, and what it means to be a gentleman. His function is as confidant to Pip. Like Biddy's, his is also a voice of common sense.

Orlick

In complete contrast to Herbert, Orlick is presented as a thoroughly **malevolent** character and Pip's enemy.

At first, Orlick's envy of Pip's favoured position in the forge seems the only motive for his hatred of Pip. Later in the novel, however, after Pip has had Orlick dismissed from Miss Havisham's employment and stated to Biddy (possibly within Orlick's hearing) that he **'would spend any money or take any pains to drive him out of that country'** *(Volume 2, Chapter 35)*, Orlick is provided with more motivation for wanting to harm Pip.

malevolent having bad intentions

Key quotations

He was a broadshouldered loose-limbed swarthy fellow of great strength, never in a hurry, and always slouching... like Cain *(Volume 1, Chapter 15)*

When I was very small and timid, he gave me to understand that the Devil lived in a black corner of the forge, and that he knew the fiend very well: also that it was necessary to make up the fire, once in seven years, with a live boy, and that I might consider myself fuel. *(Volume 1, Chapter 15)*

Orlick is described from the outside. However, we have an insight into his thoughts and feelings when he is tormenting Pip, as he holds him prisoner at the limekiln with the intention of murdering him. Here he confesses that he attacked Mrs Joe, but says Pip was responsible. He explains how being hounded out of his job forced him to find new allies and he boasts of his new relationship with Compeyson and his determination to see Magwitch dead.

Orlick's function is to act out Pip's **repressed desires**. For example, his attack on Mrs Joe puts a stop to her bullying treatment of Pip and, towards the end of the book, Orlick's humiliation and cruel treatment of Pumblechook reminds us of what Pip wanted to do to the 'swindler'.

Key quotations

I used to want—quite painfully—to burst into spiteful tears, fly at Pumblechook, and pummel him all over. *(Volume 1, Chapter 12)*

Activity 18

What do think Orlick's function is in the novel? Look at the possibilities listed in the 'Upgrade' panel at the end of this section.

Just as Compeyson is Magwitch's **nemesis**, so Orlick is Pip's.

Orlick's name is not refined; he claims his Christian name is Dolge, which Pip says is 'a clear impossibility' *(Volume 1, Chapter 15)*. He is associated with the Devil when first introduced and with the themes of social class, crime and punishment, and violence.

nemesis an arch-enemy

repressed desires feelings that people have but try to deny or hide from themselves

Minor characters

Dickens's novels are always peopled with a great many characters, both major and minor. Of the minor characters mentioned in the 'Plot and Structure' section of this book the most significant are the Pocket family, Bentley Drummle and Trabb's boy.

The minor characters fall into distinct groups. Some Pip encounters in his own village and in the main town, where Satis House is situated; others he meets in London.

The Pocket family

This family consists of Matthew Pocket, his snobbish wife Belinda and a family of eight children, including Herbert. Dickens gives Matthew the comical trait of frequently lifting himself up by the hair as a gesture of frustration. He supplies the novel's key definition of what a true gentleman is, depending upon his 'heart' rather than appearance. The Pockets are linked to the theme of parents and children.

The other branch of the Pocket family, consisting of Sarah, Camilla, Mr Camilla and Georgiana, are all intent on **ingratiating themselves** with Miss Havisham for their own gain and are much put out by Pip's good fortune, which they believe comes from Miss Havisham.

Bentley Drummle and Startop

Drummle and Startop are fellow pupils of Pip's at Matthew Pocket's educational establishment. While Startop is a rather feminine but good-natured young man, who will later support Pip and Herbert in their attempt to get Magwitch abroad, Bentley Drummle is a moody and unpleasant brute whose family are wealthy and well connected. Drummle marries Estella, then treats her cruelly. Estella's decision to throw herself away on Drummle deeply upsets Pip. Drummle, nicknamed "the Spider" by Jaggers *(Volume 2, Chapter 26)*, is linked to the themes of what it means to be a gentleman and violence.

The Aged P and Miss Skiffins

Wemmick's elderly, stone-deaf father is a delightful cameo character. He shows the tender-hearted side of Wemmick and is a model of satisfaction in old age.

Miss Skiffins is Wemmick's prim lady friend, who becomes his wife. Her sweet nature helps to show Wemmick's attachment to a more wholesome life than that lived near Newgate prison.

Other characters

Molly, Jaggers' housekeeper, is the opposite of Miss Skiffins. Not prim but a "wild beast tamed" *(Volume 3, Chapter 48)*, she is Estella's real mother and, although not convicted, a murderess.

> **ingratiate oneself** to seek approval of another person, usually in an attempt to gain some benefit

Trabb's boy plays a small role in showing how snobbish and conceited Pip has become since coming into his 'expectations'. He mocks Pip mercilessly in the street, pretending to be in great awe of him and impersonating Pip, repeating the phrase **"Don't know yah!"** *(Volume 2, Chapter 30)* in an affected voice to mock Pip's pretensions. He is linked to the theme of social class.

Clara and Bill Barley are introduced in the later stages of the novel. Clara is Herbert's pretty and amiable fiancée; Bill Barley is her irascible father, who we never see but only hear moaning and shouting at his daughter from the upper rooms of the lodging house. They are linked to the theme of parents and children.

Wopsle is the church clerk with a love of his own voice, one of Dickens's comic caricatures. Like Pip, he leaves the village to go to London, aiming to become a star actor, **'reviving the Drama'** *(Volume 3, Chapter 47)*. He does neither. He is linked to the theme of identity and social ambition.

Compeyson makes a very brief appearance at the beginning and end of the novel, on each occasion struggling to escape Magwitch's grip. He is a vital character in the story, however, as he is responsible for Miss Havisham's wasted life, Estella's damaged personality, Magwitch's life sentence in Australia, Pip's 'expectations' and Magwitch's capture. He is linked to the themes of identity, what it is to be a gentleman, crime and the law.

Activity 19

1. Using the 'Upgrade' panel at the end of this chapter as your guide, write two or more sentences about the contribution that each of the minor characters makes to the novel.

2. Use the character map at the end of this chapter as a model to group characters according to the following types:
   - orphans
   - role models
   - villains
   - friends.

Dickens's use of paired characters

Dickens sometimes appears to be presenting his characters in pairs, for example: the two contrasting convicts, one a 'gentleman' and one a 'warmint'; two father-figures for Pip in the village, Joe and Uncle Pumblechook; two further father figures in London, Jaggers and Magwitch; two potential wives for Pip, Biddy and Estella; two young men at the forge, Pip and Orlick; two young men in London, Pip and Herbert; two potential benefactors, Miss Havisham and Magwitch; and, in Wemmick, we seem to have two characters in one.

Activity 20

What effects are created by these apparent doubles in the novel? Think about the ways in which characters compare and contrast and how Dickens seems to be suggesting alternative paths at every turn. You may consider the significance of the finger-post in Pip's village.

Character map

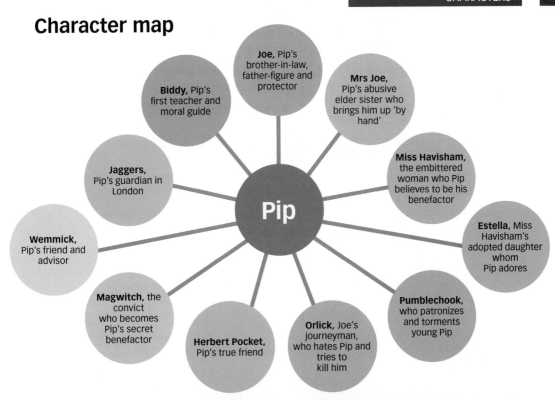

Joe, Pip's brother-in-law, father-figure and protector

Mrs Joe, Pip's abusive elder sister who brings him up 'by hand'

Biddy, Pip's first teacher and moral guide

Jaggers, Pip's guardian in London

Miss Havisham, the embittered woman who Pip believes to be his benefactor

Pip

Wemmick, Pip's friend and advisor

Estella, Miss Havisham's adopted daughter whom Pip adores

Magwitch, the convict who becomes Pip's secret benefactor

Herbert Pocket, Pip's true friend

Orlick, Joe's journeyman, who hates Pip and tries to kill him

Pumblechook, who patronizes and torments young Pip

Writing about characters

Upgrade

In your assessment you may be asked to write about one or more characters. Equally important is considering how Dickens presents the character and how he uses the character to communicate his ideas to an audience.

Always try to refer to the following methods of presentation, where applicable:

- what the character looks like/sounds like/wears
- what the character says about himself/herself and about others
- what others say about the character
- through contrast/comparison with other characters
- through what the character does, his/her actions and/or reactions in the novel
- what kind of language the character uses when speaking.

When thinking about the purpose or function of the character, you should consider the following possible uses:

- to give/receive information
- to develop the plot
- to comment on or to represent specific themes
- to act as a foil or contrast to other characters
- to alter the mood or atmosphere, for example, to add humour or pathos
- to act as a catalyst (bringing about change in the story)
- to act as a mouthpiece for the novelist's views.

Language

There are a number of striking features about Dickens's use of language in this novel:

- he adopts the narrative voice of a mature, educated man and sometimes, but not always, uses quite complicated and lengthy sentence constructions
- he creates vivid and memorable characters through descriptions of their appearance and habitual actions
- he uses much **figurative language**, including **similes** and **metaphors**, using repetition as a means of highlighting key themes and/or **motifs**
- he makes frequent allusions to other literature, including both the Old and New Testaments from the Bible
- he adopts a largely comic tone in the narrative, especially when he is presenting his caricatures; however, he is also capable of creating very touching moments
- he makes extensive use of dialogue between characters, giving the novel a dramatic quality at times
- he makes frequent references to the five senses throughout, adding to the atmosphere of the novel and helping to create a vivid impression of Pip's experiences.

figurative language any language, including metaphors and similes, that is used in a non-literal way

metaphor a word or phrase that compares one thing with another without using 'like' or 'as', e.g. 'As I watched them… enjoying themselves so much, I thought what terrible good sauce for a dinner my fugitive friend on the marshes was…'

motif a word, phrase or image repeated to create specific effects, e.g. hands in *Great Expectations*

simile figure of speech that compares one thing with another using 'like' or 'as' to highlight the similarity, e.g. 'she pounced on me like an eagle on a lamb'

The narrative voice and sentence structure

We have already considered how Dickens's use of the first-person narrative encourages the reader to sympathize with Pip. It allows him to 'speak' directly to us.

Key quotations

Whatever I acquired, I tried to impart to Joe. This statement sounds so well, that I cannot in my conscience let it pass unexplained. I wanted to make Joe less ignorant and common, that he might be worthier of my society and less open to Estella's reproach. *(Volume 1, Chapter 15)*

In the quotation above Pip not only speaks directly to us but he comments on his own writing and adds an insight into the motivations of his younger self – he steps out of the narrative voice to address us directly.

There are often two voices – that of the older, sophisticated Pip and that of the younger Pip. The two voices are reflected in the language and sentence types that Dickens uses.

In the very first chapter, Pip introduces himself, using quite simple sentence structures to begin with, before his first very long one:

Key quotations

My father's family name being Pirrip, and my Christian name Philip, my infant tongue could make of both names nothing longer or more explicit than Pip. *(26 words)*

So, I called myself Pip, and came to be called Pip. *(11 words)*

Ours was the marsh country, down by the river, within, as the river wound, twenty miles of the sea. *(19 words)*

My first most vivid and broad impression of the identity of things, seems to me to have been gained on a memorable raw afternoon towards evening. *(26 words)*

1 Dickens adds to the unfriendly feeling of the location by including the word 'bleak' and adding the detail about the nettles, which we know can sting.

2 By incorporating inscriptions typically found on headstones into the thoughts of a little boy, Dickens creates a humorous tone.

3 By naming his dead brothers, Dickens creates sympathy for them and Pip.

4 Dickens works outwards from the churchyard to beyond it; the words 'dark', 'flat' and 'wilderness' are all negative descriptions of the landscape.

5 The scope of the picture widens, zooming out like a camera.

At such a time I found out for certain that this bleak place overgrown with nettles[1] was the churchyard; and that Philip Pirrip, late of this parish, and also Georgiana wife of the above[2], were dead and buried; and that Alexander, Bartholomew, Abraham, Tobias, and Roger[3], infant children of the aforesaid[2], were also dead and buried; and that the dark flat wilderness beyond the churchyard[4], intersected with dikes and mounds and gates, with scattered cattle feeding on it, was the marshes;[5] and that the low leaden line[6] beyond, was the river; and that the distant savage lair[7] from which the wind was rushing[8], was the sea; and that the small bundle of shivers[9] growing afraid of it all and beginning to cry[10], was Pip[11].
(124 words)

6 This alliteration draws attention to the bleakness of the river.

7 This description makes the sea sound like a terrifying place, home to savagery.

8 You can almost feel the cold wind 'rushing' from the sea.

9 Dickens 'zooms' back to focus on little Pip and makes him appear very vulnerable in contrast with the vast landscape.

10 Dickens captures the fear of the little boy so we can visualize and hear his upset.

11 By referring to himself in the third person, the narrator puts 'Pip' right at the end of the sentence, making him seem more alone.

By repeating the word 'and' throughout this extract, Dickens is using a **syntetic** construction to suggest the way young children often speak before they learn more sophisticated sentence structures.

syntetic the use of conjunctions (e.g. 'and' or 'but') joining different parts of a sentence together

Pip looks at the graves of his parents and brothers

Lengthy sentences can be used for a number of different effects. Here Dickens describes Clara:

Key quotations

There was something so natural and winning in Clara's resigned way of looking at these stores in detail, as Herbert pointed them out; and something so confiding, loving, and innocent in her modest manner of yielding herself to Herbert's embracing arm; and something so gentle in her, so much needing protection on Mill Pond Bank, by Chinks's Basin, and the Old Green Copper Rope-walk, with Old Barley growling in the beam—that I would not have undone the engagement between her and Herbert, for all the money in the pocket-book I had never opened. *(Volume 3, Chapter 46)*

Although 'and' is used six times in this sentence, they are less noticeable than before. They are not being used to suggest a childlike voice but to stress how many positive qualities Clara possesses. The main focus of the sentence is Clara's sweet nature, but Dickens's reference to 'the pocket-book', placed at the end of the sentence for emphasis, brings the reader back to remembering why Pip is here.

Activity 1

Analyse the sentence below, from the end of Chapter 7 in Volume 1, making annotations on the effects that are created by the narrative voice.

Key quotations

With that, she pounced upon me, like an eagle on a lamb, and my face was squeezed into wooden bowls in sinks, and my head was put under taps of water-butts, and I was soaped, and kneaded, and towelled, and thumped, and harrowed, and rasped, until I really was quite beside myself. *(Volume 1, Chapter 7)*

Vocabulary and characterization – dialogue

Dickens chooses to use language that is complex at times to achieve particular effects. Look at this further example from Chapter 7:

> **Key quotations**
>
> There was no indispensable necessity for my communicating with Joe by letter, inasmuch as he sat beside me and we were alone. But I delivered this written communication (slate and all) with my own hand, and Joe received it as a miracle of erudition. *(44 words; Volume 1, Chapter 7)*

This could have been written much more simply and briefly as: 'I had no need to write to Joe as he sat next to me. But I passed him my slate and Joe was very impressed with the letter.' *(28 words)*

Activity 2

Answer the following questions:

a) What effect does Dickens achieve in his version that is lost in the simplified version?

b) Why does Dickens use the phrase 'indispensable necessity' instead of 'need'?

c) Why does he use 'communicating with Joe by letter' rather than 'write'?

d) What effect is created by the fact that the message is written on a slate that has to be physically passed to Joe?

e) In terms of creating comedy, why is the phrase 'Joe received it as a miracle of erudition' more effective than 'Joe was impressed'

Dickens gives some of his characters very distinctive 'voices' through the words that they speak and the ways they pronounce them. Although many of the characters, such as Miss Havisham, Estella and the Pockets, speak without any trace of a regional accent, characters such as Joe and Magwitch speak in **dialect**.

> **dialect** a regional variety of language, in which words are pronounced differently in different parts of the country or unique words are used

Key quotations

"Stay a bit. I know what you're a going to say, Pip; stay a bit! I don't deny that your sister comes the Mo-gul over us, now and again. I don't deny that she do throw us back-falls, and that she do drop down upon us heavy. At such times as when your sister is on the Ram-page, Pip," Joe sank his voice to a whisper and glanced at the door, "cander compels fur to admit that she is a Buster." *(Joe; Volume 1, Chapter 7)*

"Dear boy and Pip's comrade. I am not a going fur to tell you my life, like a song, or a story-book. But to give it you short and handy, I'll put it at once into a mouthful of English. In jail and out of jail, in jail and out of jail, in jail and out of jail. There, you've got it. That's *my* life pretty much, down to such times as I got shipped off, arter Pip stood my friend." *(Magwitch; Volume 3, Chapter 42)*

Characters who speak in dialect reveal something of their social background, their level of education and also create a very vivid impression of their characters.

Activity 3

In pairs, each 'translate' Joe's and Magwitch's statements above into the kind of English that you speak in school. Then compare the results!

When Pip speaks as a child in the earlier part of the novel, his language is unsophisticated and contrasts a great deal with the mature expression of the older Pip narrating the story.

Mrs Joe has two modes of speech. She is rude and aggressive to Pip and Joe, but can be gracious in company with Uncle Pumblechook, putting on an affected tone of politeness.

Key quotations

"Hah!" said Mrs. Joe, restoring Tickler to his station. "Churchyard, indeed! You may well say churchyard, you two." One of us, by-the-by, had not said it at all. "You'll drive *me* to the churchyard betwixt you, one of these days, and oh, a pr-r-recious pair you'd be without me!" *(Volume 1, Chapter 2)*

"You must taste," said my sister, addressing the guests with her best grace— "you must taste, to finish with, such a delightful and delicious present of Uncle Pumblechook's!" *(Volume 1, Chapter 4)*

Dickens also invents words for certain characters to use, such as Mrs Joe's "Pompeyed" *(Volume 1, Chapter 7)* for 'pampered'. He also creates memorable phrases for some characters that act almost like catchphrases, such as "what larks!" *(Volume 3, Chapter 57)* for Joe and "portable property" *(Volume 2, Chapter 24)* for Wemmick. In this way Dickens ensured that, when his readers were reading the story in instalments, they immediately recognized characters they had already 'met' in earlier 'episodes', through recognizing their individual manner of speaking.

Another method he used to make characters immediately recognizable was in giving different characters particular idiosyncrasies, for example, Mr Jaggers's habit of biting his forefinger, Miss Havisham's way of leaning her head on the crutch stick or Orlick's habit of slouching everywhere.

Dickens's theatricality

In *Great Expectations*, Dickens makes liberal use of the power of dialogue, rather than straightforward narrative, to bring his characters to life in a very vivid and immediate way.

Key quotations

"Have you heard, Joe," I asked him that evening, upon further consideration, as he smoked his pipe at the window, "who my patron was?"

"I heerd," returned Joe, "as it were not Miss Havisham, old chap."

"Did you hear who it was, Joe?"

"Well! I heerd as it were a person what sent the person what giv' you the banknotes at the Jolly Bargemen, Pip."

"So it was."

"Astonishing!" said Joe, in the placidest way.

(Volume 3, Chapter 57)

Activity 4

Take the short exchange of dialogue above and turn it into reported speech. What is lost in the new version?

Figurative language, symbolism and motifs

Dickens chooses to use metaphors, symbolism and motifs throughout *Great Expectations* to reflect his themes and bring out his characters.

Hammers

One motif that occurs frequently is the use of the word 'hammer'. It is one of the tools of Joe's trade and so there are several references to Joe in the forge simply using his hammer, for example, when he is helping the soldiers with their faulty handcuffs: 'Then Joe began to hammer and clink, hammer and clink, and we all looked on' *(Volume 1, Chapter 5)*.

symbol a word or object used to represent a different word or object, e.g. Dickens frequently uses 'chain' to suggest oppressive duties

Later, when Joe is telling Pip why he had had no schooling, he uses the word 'hammer' in a metaphorical way:

> **Key quotations**
>
> "My father, Pip, he were given to drink, and when he were overtook with drink, he hammered away at my mother, most onmerciful. It were a'most the only hammering he did, indeed, 'xcepting at myself. And he hammered at me with a wigor only to be equalled by the wigor with which he didn't hammer at his anwil." *(Volume 1, Chapter 7)*

The hammer is also associated with Orlick and the following example shows Dickens using the word literally and figuratively at the same time:

The hammer is one of the tools of a blacksmith's trade

> **Key quotations**
>
> ...Orlick plunged at the furnace, drew out a red-hot bar, made at me with it as if he were going to run it through my body, whisked it round my head, laid it on the anvil, hammered it out—as if it were I, I thought, and the sparks were my spirting blood—and finally said, when he had hammered himself hot and the iron cold, and he again leaned on his hammer:
> "Now, master!" *(Volume 1, Chapter 15)*

After Mrs Joe's devastating beating, she draws a hammer on her slate, to signify that she wants to see Orlick, a sign that Biddy interprets:

> **Key quotations**
>
> "Why, of course!" cried Biddy, with an exultant face. "Don't you see? It's *him*!"
> Orlick, without a doubt! She had lost his name, and could only signify him by his hammer. We told him why we wanted him to come into the kitchen, and he slowly laid down his hammer, wiped his brow with his arm, took another wipe at it with his apron, and came slouching out... *(Volume 1, Chapter 16)*

The hammer sign here is used to symbolize Orlick. Dickens uses the word again in a simile to describe Joe: 'I have often thought him since, like the steam-hammer that can crush a man or pat an egg-shell, in his combination of strength with gentleness' *(Volume 1, Chapter 18)*.

And, when Magwitch quizzes Pip about the identity of his benefactor, Dickens uses the word metaphorically, once more, creating a sense of cohesion across the novel:

'With my heart beating like a heavy hammer of disordered action, I rose out of my chair, and stood with my hand upon the back of it, looking wildly at him.' *(Volume 2, Chapter 39).*

A final ironic use occurs when Dickens locates Matthew Pocket's educational establishment in Hammersmith. Here Pip is supposed to acquire the education to make him into a gentleman, rather than a smith working with his hammer in a forge.

Light and darkness

References to darkness, associated with blindness to the truth and self-delusion, are particularly prominent. Sometimes the darkness may be illuminated with candles or gaslight. The fact that Miss Havisham has blocked out the light from all the windows and lives permanently in a darkened house is both literal – she lives in darkness and artificial light – and metaphorical – she gropes around in the darkness of her own thoughts and feelings, blocking out all possibility of recovering a 'normal' life.

Pip's dream that Miss Havisham intends for him **'to restore the desolate house, admit the sunshine into the dark rooms, set the clocks a-going and the cold hearths a-blazing, tear down the cobwebs, destroy the vermin—in short, do all the shining deeds of the young Knight of romance, and marry the Princess'** *(Volume 2, Chapter 29)* turns out to be wishful thinking, based on illusions that have been encouraged in that darkened house.

The mature Pip later reflects on the consequences of Miss Havisham's irrational action in trying to stop time, seeing **'that, in shutting out the light of day, she had shut out infinitely more; that, in seclusion, she had secluded herself from a thousand natural and healing influences; that, her mind, brooding solitary, had grown diseased, as all minds do and must and will that reverse the appointed order of their Maker'** *(Volume 3, Chapter 49).*

Tips for assessment

Upgrade

The quotation above demonstrates **tripling**, another common feature of Dickens's writing. First, he refers to three things that Miss Havisham has done: she has (1) shut out the light, (2) secluded herself and (3) brooded, 'solitary'. He then uses another triple to emphasize his point: 'as all minds (1) do and (2) must and (3) will'.

Make sure you can identify this technique when you are writing about Dickens's use of language in your assessment. Its purpose is to add emphasis to the points he is making. Remember that Dickens's novels were frequently read aloud in their serial form and tripling is a device that adds rhythm and sometimes also comedy to a sentence.

tripling a device where a writer groups statements, verbs, nouns or adjectives into sequences of three to create an emphatic or comical effect, e.g. 'But there was a calm, a rest, a virtuous hush'

Just before Magwitch makes his reappearance at the end of Volume 2, Dickens depicts a particularly dark night. The lamps have all blown out around Pip's apartment and he goes out onto the staircase in the darkness.

> **Key quotations**
>
> Remembering then, that the staircase-lights were blown out, I took up my reading-lamp and went out to the stair-head. Whoever was below had stopped on seeing my lamp, for all was quiet.
>
> > "There is some one down there, is there not?" I called out, looking down.
> > "Yes," said a voice from the darkness beneath.
> > "What floor do you want?"
> > "The top. Mr. Pip." *(Volume 2, Chapter 39)*

Ironically, in the dark Pip is about to be 'enlightened' about the real identity of his benefactor. In this way, Dickens uses light and darkness both literally and metaphorically. He also makes frequent references to the mists around Pip's village in a symbolic way to suggest Pip's inability to see clearly.

Hanging and punishment

From his first meeting with Magwitch on the marshes, Pip's life is associated with crime and deadly punishment, and he is unable to shake it off. One of the many strands of Dickens's imagery in the novel is to do with hanging figures. The first example is in Volume 1, Chapter 1:

> **Key quotations**
>
> On the edge of the river I could faintly make out the only two black things in all the prospect that seemed to be standing upright; one of these was the beacon... the other, a **gibbet** with some chains hanging to it which had once held a pirate. The man was limping on towards this latter, as if he were the pirate come to life, and come down, and going back to hook himself up again. It gave me a terrible turn when I thought so... *(Volume 1, Chapter 1).*

Later in the novel, Pip twice thinks that he sees the figure of Miss Havisham 'hanging' by the neck from a beam in one of the outbuildings of Satis House and on his first day in London he finds himself at Newgate prison where he is shown, **'the Debtors' Door, out of which culprits came to be hanged'** *(Volume 2, Chapter 20)*.

These references to hanging seem to **foreshadow** Magwitch's death sentence – hanging – at the end of the novel, which he manages to evade by dying 'naturally' of his injuries.

Pip is consistently disturbed by the two death masks/casts on the shelf in Jaggers's office, which appear, in Pip's lively imagination, to be somehow communicating with him. First he simply notices **'two dreadful casts on a shelf, of faces peculiarly swollen, and twitchy about the nose'** *(Volume 2, Chapter 20)*. Then, when Pip

> **foreshadowing** (or proleptic irony) when a character says or experiences something that becomes significant later in the novel
>
> **gibbet** a scaffold built for the purpose of hanging criminals

visits Jaggers on his coming of age, they acquire an even more sinister appearance: 'their expression was as if they were making a stupid apoplectic attempt to attend to the conversation' *(Volume 2, Chapter 36)*. Once Magwitch returns to England, and Pip goes to see Jaggers, he is again unnerved by the death masks, which in the flickering firelight 'look as if they were playing a diabolical game at bo-peep with me' *(Volume 3, Chapter 48)*.

Dickens has created the effect that these inanimate, yet grisly, masks know more about Pip's benefactor than they are able to tell (as they cannot speak). At first, Pip is simply disturbed by their dreadful appearance, but as he knows the outcome of his 'expectations', the mature Pip allows us to see the masks as somehow warning Pip of what is to come. Like the visions of the hanging figures, this is another example of foreshadowing.

Hands

Another repeated motif is Dickens's references to hands. From the first chapter of the novel, where Pip describes Magwitch 'picking his way among the nettles… as if he were eluding the hands of the dead people, stretching up cautiously out of their graves, to get a twist upon his ankle and pull him in', to the final paragraph of the book, where Pip recounts, 'I took her hand in mine', Dickens repeatedly draws the reader's attention to characters' hands.

Hands are one of the most expressive parts of the human body and Dickens is able to convey a great deal about characters through describing their hands touching others, beating others, praying, pointing, stroking, boxing, shaking, rowing, putting out flames.

Sometimes Dickens presents hands realistically, for example, when describing Biddy's hands as 'always clean' *(Volume 1, Chapter 17)*. Sometimes they are used comically, for example, when Pumblechook insists on shaking Pip's hands, time after time, with the obsequious question, "May I?" *(Volume 1, Chapter 19)*.

Hands are also presented figuratively. For example, Magwitch reflects, 'a poor tool I was in his [Compeyson's] hands' *(Volume 3, Chapter 42)*. And they are used symbolically. For example in Volume 1, Chapter 8, Estella's humiliating reference to Pip's "coarse hands" becomes a symbol of his status as 'a common labouring-boy' and a source of dissatisfaction with his life at the forge.

There are references to 'bound hands' and 'manacled hands' *(Volume 1, Chapter 5)* when Pip watches Magwitch and Compeyson struggling in the ditch and, when Pip saves Miss Havisham from the fire, he looks down to see that 'both my hands were burnt' *(Volume 3, Chapter 49)*. One of Jaggers's signature actions each evening is 'washing his hands with his scented soap' *(Volume 2, Chapter 26)* as if to wash away the taint of crime that occupies his working day.

Jaggers takes delight in showing off Molly's hands and wrists and tells his dinner guests, "I have had occasion to notice many hands; but I never saw stronger in that respect, man's or woman's, than these" *(Volume 2, Chapter 26)*. The next time he sees Molly, Pip is suddenly struck with the realization that Estella has 'exactly such eyes and such hands' *(Volume 3, Chapter 48)* and that Molly must be Estella's birth mother. And when Pip tells Wemmick and Jaggers that Magwitch is Estella's father, Jaggers uses a grisly image, warning Pip that it would be better to "chop off that bandaged left hand of yours with your bandaged right hand, and then pass the chopper on to Wemmick there, to cut *that* off too" *(Volume 3, Chapter 51)* than to reveal Estella's parentage to her.

Magwitch is repeatedly described reaching out for Pip's hands when he first returns from New South Wales.

Key quotations

As he ascended the last stair or two, and the light of my lamp included us both, I saw, with a stupid kind of amazement, that he was holding out both his hands to me. *(Volume 2, Chapter 39)*

He came back to where I stood, and again held out both his hands. Not knowing what to do—for, in my astonishment I had lost my self-possession—I reluctantly gave him my hands. He grasped them heartily, raised them to his lips, kissed them, and still held them. *(Volume 2, Chapter 39)*

At first, Pip's blood runs cold at Magwitch's show of affection for him, but by the time Magwitch has been captured and sentenced to death, Pip has come to appreciate his loyalty, pitying his wretched life and caring for him in return, holding his hand throughout his trial and on his death-bed.

Key quotations

He had spoken his last words. He smiled, and I understood his touch to mean that he wished to lift my hand, and lay it on his breast. I laid it there, and he smiled again, and put both his hands upon it. *(Volume 3, Chapter 56)*

With a last faint effort, which would have been powerless but for my yielding to it and assisting it, he raised my hand to his lips. Then, he gently let it sink upon his breast again, with his own hands lying on it. The placid look at the white ceiling came back, and passed away, and his head dropped quietly on his breast. *(Volume 3, Chapter 56)*

Activity 5

Which of the examples above uses hands realistically and which symbolically? Work in pairs to decide.

The five senses

Dickens makes frequent reference to the senses of touch, taste, smell, sight and hearing throughout the novel, bringing Pip's world vividly to life.

He uses the word 'touch' or 'touching' explicitly nearly 70 times to depict developing relationships such as the friendship between Pip and Wemmick or Pip and Herbert. Some of Miss Havisham's first words to Pip revolve around her touching her **"Broken!"** heart *(Volume 1, Chapter 8)*

Pip didn't enjoy his Christmas dinner

and Estella's **'friendly touch'** *(Volume 3, Chapter 59)* is one of the last sensations that Pip describes.

Although the word 'taste' appears less frequently, Dickens describes many meals and drinks in the course of the book, starting with Magwitch hungrily devouring the **"broken wittles"** *(Volume 1, Chapter 5)*; then Christmas lunch at the forge with ample gravy and plum pudding; dining with Herbert and later with the Pockets; taking dinner with Jaggers; enjoying tea and toast with Wemmick; not forgetting the memorable taste of 'tar-water' and its remarkable effect on Uncle Pumblechook.

There are innumerable references to eyes and many to sight. Sometimes Dickens writes ironically about Pip's view of the world; he does not always see clearly, he does not base his ideas on hard evidence as Jaggers advises and sometimes he 'sees' things that are not there.

There are some specific references to smells: the airless smell of Miss Havisham's house; the fustiness of Uncle Pumblechook's establishment; the smell of fire and burning; the smell of the blackcurrant leaf that Biddy tears up as she talks to Pip; the stench of Smithfield, **'all asmear with filth and fat and blood and foam'** *(Volume 2, Chapter 20)*. The smell most frequently referred to is that of Jaggers's scented soap with which he washes away, as far as he can, his involvement with the criminals he deals with.

Sounds are important throughout: the sound of guns announcing an escaped prisoner from the Hulks; the sound of church bells and the bells on the cattle in the marshland; the sound of the anvil and of the voices that sing 'Old Clem'; the sound of Pumblechook's mare **"ringing like a peal of bells"** *(Volume 1, Chapter 7)*; the sound of Joe's 'clumsy' footsteps on the staircase of Barnard's Inn; and the sound of Magwitch's **'footstep on the stair'** *(Volume 2, Chapter 39)* in Pip's new lodgings in the Temple.

Activity 6

Find other examples of Dickens's writing appealing to the reader's senses.

> ### Tips for assessment
>
> Remember when you are working on an extract-based assessment task to be alert to the presence and meaning of some of Dickens's key motifs – the hammer, light and dark, visions of hanging, hands, the five senses. Be sure to include reference to their significance in your answers.

Dickens's comic tone

There is some comedy in the situation that Dickens presents in *Great Expectations*: a poor boy gets rich through the determined efforts of a criminal he once helped, whilst believing that his money comes from an eccentric, wealthy lady. However, the real comedy is not Pip's story but in the way that Dickens tells it.

Dickens's comical caricatures go a long way to creating the light-hearted comic tone of the novel but it is also created by the narrator's lightness of touch. Although Pip often recalls painful memories, especially when he writes about his hopeless love for Estella and his guilty conscience over abandoning Joe, he succeeds in making the reader laugh on many occasions. One of the ways he does this is to talk directly to us, in the present and as an **aside** to his narrative, when he is writing about the past.

> **Key quotations**
>
> "Churchyard, indeed! You may well say churchyard, you two." One of us, by-the-by, had not said it at all. *(Volume 1, Chapter 2)*
>
> "And couldn't Uncle Pumblechook, being always considerate and thoughtful for us—though you may not think it, Joseph," in a tone of the deepest reproach, as if he were the most callous of nephews, "then mention this boy, standing Prancing here"—which I solemnly declare I was not doing—"that I have for ever been a willing slave to?" *(Volume 1, Chapter 7)*

> **aside** a remark by a character in a play, made directly to the audience, which the other characters supposedly do not hear

Another aspect of the prevailing comic tone allows the older Pip to make wry observations about other characters with the benefit of hindsight. For example, when Pip comments on Joe's inability to recognize any letter other than more Js and Os, he concludes, 'I derived from this, that Joe's education, like Steam, was yet in its infancy' *(Volume 1, Chapter 7)*, a remark that the seven-year-old Pip would obviously have been incapable of making.

Pip is even able to see the funny side of his sister's attack and her funeral.

> **Key quotations**
>
> ...I became aware of my sister—lying without sense or movement on the bare boards where she had been knocked down by a tremendous blow... destined never to be on the Rampage again, while she was the wife of Joe. *(Volume 1, Chapter 15)*
>
> ...I became conscious of the servile Pumblechook in a black cloak and several yards of hatband, who was alternately stuffing himself, and making obsequious movements to catch my attention. The moment he succeeded, he came over to me (breathing sherry and crumbs), and said in a subdued voice, "May I, dear sir?" and did.
> *(Volume 2, Chapter 35)*

Tips for assessment

Be sure to mention Dickens's ability to find humour in even the darkest of subjects in your assessments.

Other comic interludes include Pip's humiliating encounter with Trabb's boy, who mocks him mercilessly for his snobbish behaviour, and Pip's first visit to Matthew Pocket's home where he finds the Pocket children 'tumbling up' *(Volume 2, Chapter 22)*.

Activity 7

Choose your favourite comic episode from the novel and select a paragraph or so. Annotate the paragraphs to show how Dickens has created the comedy, using the situation, the characters or comical turns of phrase.

Writing about language

Remember, particularly when you are asked to comment on an extract from the novel, to include reference to the following aspects:

- Dickens's careful choice and use of language; his use of short and longer sentences and the effects he is aiming to achieve
- his use of repetition and figurative language to emphasize themes and motifs
- the ways he creates sympathy for Pip through his narrative technique
- his creation of individual 'voices' for his characters, including those who speak in regional accents and dialect
- Dickens's creation of comedy through his direct address to the reader and his comical presentation of caricatures.

Themes

In previous sections, there has already been mention of a number of key themes in *Great Expectations* and in this section we will explore some of the most important ones and how Dickens presents them. Themes can be found in repeated events in the plot, in similarities and differences between particular characters, and in repeated images and motifs in the language of a text.

Prominent themes emerge in the following ways:

- the content/plotlines of the novel: Pip grows up and becomes a gentleman
- when characters discuss a theme: Pip discusses becoming a gentleman with Biddy; Herbert and Pip discuss whether or not Compeyson is a 'gentleman'
- when characters, through their actions, 'do' the theme: Joe behaves as a gentleman throughout the novel, despite his lack of polish and education
- when the theme is conveyed through repeated motifs and/or in figurative language: clothes are often described as the outer show of a gentleman, sometime concealing the true qualities of the man wearing them
- when the theme is linked or contrasted to another theme: the 'gentleman' theme is linked to identity
- when a character acts as a mouthpiece for the novelist's views on the theme: Matthew Pocket's pronouncement on the need for a true gentleman to be a gentleman **"at heart"** *(Volume 2, Chapter 22)*.

Identity

The theme of identity is apparent in the presentation of several characters. However, the concept of 'identity' is slightly different from that of 'character' because it implies how a person is perceived by others rather than simply who they are. It can also be used to indicate what an individual wants to, or tries to, be seen as. For example, we could describe Jaggers as a forceful 'character'. However, Dickens makes it plain that Jaggers has constructed his identity to intimidate others and that is why he bites his finger and points it at those he is 'bullying' or flourishes his handkerchief before he speaks. In Volume 2, Chapter 24, Pip tells us that Jaggers **'never laughed'** and he tells Wemmick that he **'hardly knew what to make of'** Jaggers. Wemmick replies, **"Tell him that, and he'll take it as a compliment"** because he knows that Jaggers has intentionally cultivated this forbidding exterior identity to exploit in his profession as a lawyer.

The theme of identity is principally explored through Pip's development. Before he visits Satis House, Pip is presented as an ordinary boy for the times, learning to read and write, doing odd jobs in the village, attending evening classes, bullied by his sister but protected by Joe. All this changes when Estella gives him a new perception of his identity as a **'common labouring-boy'** *(Volume 1, Chapter 8)*. From this point, he embarks on a plan of self-improvement and begins to dream of transforming himself into a 'gentleman'.

Pip is disappointed that Miss Havisham shows no interest in his ambition to improve his education. In fact, she paves the way for Pip's early apprenticeship to Joe. Pip's unhappiness with his new position as blacksmith's apprentice is linked with his fear of what Estella would think of him if she saw him at work in the forge.

> **Key quotations**
>
> What I dreaded was, that in some unlucky hour I, being at my grimiest and commonest, should lift up my eyes and see Estella looking in at one of the wooden windows of the forge. I was haunted by the fear that she would, sooner or later, find me out, with a black face and hands, doing the coarsest part of my work, and would exult over me and despise me.
> *(Volume 1, Chapter 14)*

Pip looked the gentleman in his new clothes

When Jaggers brings the news of Pip's startling change of fortune, Pip is able to begin to construct the identity of a gentleman he has been dreaming of since meeting Estella. Pip's first action is to order new clothes so that he can present himself to the world as a gentleman and, once in London and with the help of Matthew and Herbert Pocket, he learns the manners, pastimes and conversation appropriate to the gentleman he is determined to appear.

Magwitch's return and revelation that he is Pip's benefactor throws Pip into confusion as he realizes that his status as a gentleman is built on the earnings of a criminal rather than on the inherited wealth of Miss Havisham. At first he feels contaminated by contact with Magwitch but as he comes to understand his patron more fully, Pip accepts a new identity as 'son' to Magwitch, who he comes to care for with tender regard until his death.

Pip's reconstructed identity is complete after his illness and reunion with Joe and Biddy. As a respectable partner in Clarriker's firm, he earns his own living and the final chapter suggests that this now real gentleman will be rewarded with the prize of Estella.

> **Activity 1**
>
> Pip says that he does not recognize himself from the following description. Do you? Look back over the novel and find one example of each of the qualities that Herbert identifies.

"You call me a lucky fellow. Of course, I am. I was a blacksmith's boy but yesterday; I am—what shall I say I am—to-day?"

"Say a good fellow, if you want a phrase," returned Herbert, smiling, and clapping his hand on the back of mine, "a good fellow, with **impetuosity** and hesitation, boldness and **diffidence**, action and dreaming, curiously mixed in him." *(Volume 2, Chapter 30)*

diffidence a shy, hesitant approach to life

impetuosity a tendency to act impulsively

The theme of identity is also explored through other characters in the novel. Miss Havisham has defined herself as a 'jilted bride' ever since Compeyson abandoned her and everything she has done since has contributed to that identity. Like Pip, she has constructed her own identity, frozen in time and place to the moment when, dressing for her wedding, she received Compeyson's letter.

Miss Havisham has also constructed Estella's identity. Herbert describes Estella as "hard and haughty and capricious to the last degree... brought up by Miss Havisham to wreak revenge on all the male sex" *(Volume 2, Chapter 22)*. Estella coldly tells her adoptive mother, "I am what you have made me." *(Volume 2, Chapter 38)* Only Bentley Drummle's cruel treatment destroys her constructed identity; as she tells Pip, "I have been bent and broken, but—I hope—into a better shape" *(Volume 3, Chapter 59)*.

Magwitch is the product of a social system that offered no assistance to a starving orphan other than prison. Branded as 'hardened' by the world, by degrees he came to be hardened, violent and dangerous. By contrast, Compeyson constructed the identity of a smooth-talking and apparently educated gentleman, an outward appearance that deceived the judge at his trial.

"This is the way it was, that when I was a ragged little creetur as much to be pitied as ever I see... I got the name of being hardened. 'This is a terrible hardened one,' they says to prison wisitors, picking out me." *(Volume 3, Chapter 42)*

"When we was put in the dock, I noticed first of all what a gentleman Compeyson looked, wi' his curly hair and his black clothes and his white pocket-handkercher, and what a common sort of a wretch I looked." *(Volume 3, Chapter 42)*

Dickens draws attention to the contrast in the constructed identities of the two accused men in the dock and shows how appearances can be deceptive.

Wemmick is another character associated with the theme of identity as he has deliberately set out to create one identity for the office and the other for Walworth. This is emphasized when Pip has dinner with Jaggers, with Wemmick as a second guest. Pip describes Wemmick being 'as dry and distant to me as if there were twin Wemmicks and this was the wrong one' (Volume 3, Chapter 48). Later, in Volume 3, Chapter 51, when Jaggers learns from Pip about Wemmick's 'old father' and Wemmick's 'pleasant and playful ways', he accuses Wemmick of being 'the most cunning impostor in all London'.

In these examples, Dickens explores the theme of 'identity' through plot and characterization. This theme is also linked to the theme of social class.

Activity 2

Look at the following short extracts and write a sentence or two explaining how they relate to the theme of identity.

Key quotations

As I stood opposite to Mr. Pocket, Junior, delivering him the bags, One, Two, I saw the starting appearance come into his own eyes that I knew to be in mine, and he said falling back:

"Lord bless me, you're the prowling boy!"

"And you," said I, "are the pale young gentleman!"
(Volume 2, Chapter 21)

Next day the clothes I had ordered, all came home, and he put them on. Whatever he put on, became him less (it dismally seemed to me) than what he had worn before. To my thinking, there was something in him that made it hopeless to attempt to disguise him. The more I dressed him and the better I dressed him, the more he looked like the slouching fugitive on the marshes... and... from head to foot there was Convict in the very grain of the man. (Volume 3, Chapter 40)

Social class and what it means to be a 'gentleman'

Closely linked to the theme of identity is Dickens's exploration of what it means to be a 'gentleman', a theme we have already noticed through examining Dickens's methods of comparing and contrasting characters.

Dickens presents several examples of characters who could be considered to be gentlemen. In terms of their social class, their birth and family, Matthew Pocket, Herbert Pocket, Bentley Drummle and Startop are gentlemen.

Compeyson has the outward appearance of a gentleman only. His 'profession' of forgery and counterfeiting, and his deceit of Miss Havisham, reveal him to be no such thing, as Matthew Pocket says:

Key quotations

"... no man who was not a true gentleman at heart, ever was, since the world began, a true gentleman in manner... no varnish can hide the grain of the wood; and... the more varnish you put on, the more the grain will express itself." *(Volume 2, Chapter 22)*

Magwitch's experience of Compeyson's trickery has given him a poor view of 'gentlemen'. Nevertheless, Magwitch determines to make Pip a gentleman, partly to reward him for bringing him food on the marshes and partly to take revenge on the class that has persecuted him.

Key quotations

"You acted noble, my boy," said he. "Noble, Pip! And I have never forgot it!" *(Volume 2, Chapter 39)*

"I've come to the old country fur to see my gentleman spend his money *like* a gentleman. That'll be *my* pleasure. *My* pleasure 'ull be fur to see him do it. And blast you all!" he wound up, looking round the room and snapping his fingers once with a loud snap, "blast you every one, from the judge in his wig, to the colonist a stirring up the dust, I'll show a better gentleman than the whole kit on you put together!" *(Volume 3, Chapter 40)*

Magwitch doesn't notice the 'frenzy of fear and dislike' that this outburst has caused Pip although he does recognize that he had been 'low' *(Volume 3, Chapter 40)* and he vows not to repeat his lowness. There is both comedy and pathos in this promise, as Magwitch cannot avoid appearing 'low' to Pip with his coarse manners and uneducated speech.

Pip originally wanted to move out of his social class and become a 'gentleman' to make himself an acceptable suitor to Estella. He mistakenly thought that Miss Havisham had given him a fortune partly for that reason. His discovery that Magwitch is his real patron fills him with horror, not only because of Magwitch's criminal past but also because it means that Estella was never part of his 'expectations'. When Magwitch promises to 'buy' for Pip the 'bright eyes somewhere wot you love the thoughts on', Pip's internalized words 'O Estella, Estella!' *(Volume 2, Chapter 39)* reveal the end of that "poor dream" *(Volume 3, Chapter 59)*. Little does Pip or the reader know, at this point, that Magwitch will turn out to be Estella's father.

The real 'gentleman' of the novel turns out to be Joe, despite his lack of education and polish, because he practises the Christian virtues of patience and forgiveness, values his 'fellow man' and always seeks to do good in his life.

> **Key quotations**
>
> "And, dear Joe, you have the best wife in the whole world, and she will make you as happy as even you deserve to be, you dear, good, noble Joe!" *(Volume 3, Chapter 58)*

Activity 3

Does Pip become a gentleman through his 'expectations' or through his experiences? You might consider the education he receives from Herbert and Matthew Pocket as part of his 'expectations' as well as his introduction to the power of money. His life experiences include mixing with people of a higher class than himself; befriending Wemmick; and meeting characters such as the Aged P and Miss Skiffins. The way he reacts to Magwitch's return also helps to shape him. Debate this in small groups.

This theme is linked to the themes of love and loyalty, to education, as well as to Christian virtues.

Children and parents

Dickens presents this theme in two main ways, through characterization and plot.

At the beginning of the 19th century, life expectancy was much shorter than today and being orphaned was a relatively common occurrence. Many women died in childbirth and many children died in infancy. So Pip's situation, as he looks at the graves of his parents and little brothers at the opening of the novel, does not make him an extraordinary child for the times.

Dickens invites us to consider the effects of proper parenting, partly through his presentation of three orphans of about the same age – Pip, Estella and Biddy.

Neither Pip nor Estella has any recollection of their real parents and both have unconventional childhoods. Pip's elder sister is violent with him and Joe can only do so much to protect him. When Joe is nursing Pip through his illness towards the end of the novel, he reveals his guilt at not being able to stop Mrs Joe from beating Pip.

Even though she does not bring him up, Miss Haversham has a profound effect on Pip's young life

> **Key quotations**
>
> "Lookee here, old chap," said Joe. "I done what I could to keep you and Tickler in sunders, but my power were not always fully equal to my inclinations. For when your poor sister had a mind to drop into you, it were notsermuch... that she dropped into me too, if I put myself in opposition to her but that she dropped into you always heavier for it."
> *(Volume 3, Chapter 57)*

Although Pip's sister was cruel, Pip learned gentleness and moral values through his companionship with Joe.

Estella had no such balance in her young life and although Jaggers hoped to save her from the miseries of poverty and Miss Havisham hoped to save her from heartbreak like her own, Estella grew up in a darkened house, raised by a woman obsessed with her own abandonment to be cold, proud, scornful and incapable of love.

Pip first describes Biddy as 'an orphan like myself', adding 'like me, too, had been brought up by hand. She was most noticeable, I thought, in respect of her extremities; for, her hair always wanted brushing, her hands always wanted washing, and her shoes always wanted mending and pulling up at heel' *(Volume 1, Chapter 7)*. Biddy lived with her grandmother and, despite her apparent neglect, she develops into a caring and intelligent young woman who makes the best of herself for its own sake rather than with any notion of acquiring great status.

Biddy nurses Mrs Joe in her incapacity, patiently accepts Pip's transformation from pupil to 'gentleman', recognizes Joe's worth and is fully contented to fill her place as his wife at the forge. Dickens leaves the reader secure in the sense that both Joe and Biddy will be effective and affectionate parents to their little son and daughter despite the role models in their own childhoods.

Other 'children' are not so fortunate. Both Joe and Magwitch have the opportunity to talk about their childhoods. Joe's father was an alcoholic, violent when drunk and lazy when sober. Magwitch never knew his parents and his earliest memory was being abandoned by the adult figure in his life: "a tinker—and he'd took the fire with him, and left me wery cold" *(Volume 3, Chapter 42)*. Magwitch took to crime as a way of survival. Pip was lucky to have found a home with Joe and his sister at the forge, avoiding a similar fate.

Even the comparatively wealthy Pocket parents, with several servants and children's maids to assist them, are shown to be doing a poor job of raising their children. Although Herbert has turned out well, the rest of the children are 'tumbling up' and forever in danger of "bouncing" into the river and being "drownded" *(Volume 2, Chapter 22)*. The Pocket parents are not vicious, but simply incompetent.

These examples focus on the effects of parents on their children as they are growing up, but Dickens also gives us two examples of adult children caring for their parents.

Wemmick's tender care of his Aged P is one of the most touching aspects of the novel as we see the Aged P being cosseted by his son, indulged in his simple pleasures, kept warm, clean and well fed. The Aged P, in return, appears to worship his son, admires his domestic cleverness and is immensely proud of him.

By contrast, we see Herbert's fiancée, Clara, caring for old 'Gruffandgrim' with little evident gratitude in return. Bill Barley, whom Herbert also calls **"an unconscionable old shark"** *(Volume 3, Chapter 46)* is about as unlike Wemmick's Aged P as can be imagined. He tyrannizes his daughter and spends his time in bed, drinking rum and eating spicy food, both of which inflame his gout and make him short-tempered.

> **Key quotations**
>
> **"He keeps his grog ready-mixed in a little tub on the table. Wait a moment, and you'll hear Clara lift him up to take some.—There he goes!" Another roar, with a prolonged shake at the end.** *(Volume 3, Chapter 46)*

Nevertheless, Clara looks after her father dutifully and, although Herbert seems to be counting the days until Bill Barley's **"pegging"** *(Volume 3, Chapter 50)* days are over, Clara herself seems completely devoted to her father.

> **Activity 4**
>
> Look again at Chapters 25 and 37 in Volume 2 and Chapter 45 and 55 in Volume 3. How important do you think the Aged P is in the novel? You should think about his pride in his son's achievements, the simplicity and wholesomeness of his routine, and his contribution to the comic nature of the book.

Pip sees 'his' convict arrested by soldiers

This theme is also linked to the theme of love and loyalty.

Crime, punishment and the law

Throughout the novel, Dickens explores the theme of crime, punishment and the operation of the law. He invites the reader to consider why some people commit crimes and how fairly criminals are treated once convicted. He also explores the corruption that exists in the 'justice' system. The theme is presented in three different ways, through the plot, through characterization and through Dickens's choice of language.

Pip's life includes several brushes with the criminal world that he finds shocking or disturbing. For example, as a boy, Pip meets two violent, escaped convicts as well as the 'secret-looking' man *(Volume 1, Chapter 10)* who stirs his rum with Joe's file. He joins the party of soldiers on the hunt for Magwitch and Compeyson, and sees them arrested, manacled and taken back to the Hulks.

In London, he sees some of Jaggers's desperate clients as well as a number of false witnesses, paid to swear to 'anythink' *(Volume 2, Chapter 20)* and Wemmick shows him a condemned man, who Pip refers to as a 'dead plant' *(Volume 2, Chapter 32)*. At Jaggers's house, Pip meets Molly, a jealous murderess whom Jaggers got acquitted and has tamed. Even before Magwitch returns and claims him as his 'son', Pip muses on the ways in which 'prison and crime' *(Volume 2, Chapter 32)* have been part of the fabric of his existence.

Key quotations

… how strange it was that I should be encompassed by all this taint of prison and crime; that, in my childhood… I should have first encountered it; that, it should have reappeared on two occasions, starting out like a stain that was faded but not gone; that, it should in this new way pervade my fortune and advancement. *(Volume 2, Chapter 32)*

In this way, Pip's association with crime is established through the plotline.

Although Pip does not realize it, Magwitch is not only responsible for causing him to steal and to conceal his 'crime' in taking the 'wittles' and file, but also for bringing him into regular contact with the world of crime and punishment by appointing Jaggers as Pip's guardian in London. Jaggers's office is 'greasy' with the shoulders of criminals 'shuffling' against the walls *(Volume 2, Chapter 24)*. Its proximity to Newgate prison makes it the first place in London that Pip sees – and a 'sickening' *(Volume 2, Chapter 20)* place he finds it.

His first impressions of London cause Pip to enquire innocently of Wemmick if London is "a very wicked place" to which Wemmick replies, darkly, "You may get cheated, robbed, and murdered, in London. But there are plenty of people anywhere, who'll do that for you." *(Volume 2, Chapter 21)*

Ironically, Wemmick's comment is entirely applicable to Pip's own village where the wickedest person of Pip's whole acquaintance actually worked alongside him at the forge. There's no need to go to Newgate to see wickedness when it exists in Joe's journeyman Orlick. Unlike Magwitch, who turned to crime for survival and who is shown to have several good qualities – gratitude, loyalty, industriousness and generosity – Orlick is presented as surly and vicious from the first time we meet him and Dickens appears to suggest that he is an example of someone **innately** bad.

innate natural; present from birth

Pip's memory of Magwitch as **'a desperately violent man'** *(Volume 2, Chapter 39)* causes him to shrink from him when he reappears as his benefactor. His recollection of the fear of Magwitch he felt when he was little prevents Pip from understanding Magwitch's gratitude to him. It had **"Never, never!"** *(Volume 2, Chapter 39)* occurred to him that the man who threatened to cut Pip's throat, eat his cheeks and get at his **'heart, and at his liver'** *(Volume 1, Chapter 1)* could ever have been the source of his 'expectations'.

Activity 5

Can Pip be blamed for never considering that Magwitch was behind his 'expectations'? In pairs, make a list of the evidence that Pip has ignored. You should look at Dickens's use of language linked to crime and punishment as you gather your examples.

Through the creation of various criminal characters Dickens presents the theme of crime and punishment in a vivid way.

Key facts about Dickens's interest in prison and punishment

Dickens was personally interested in prisons and punishments, and was actively involved in seeking to reform the way that prisoners were treated. He believed that prisoners were entitled to be treated humanely and he was fiercely opposed to both capital and corporal punishment.

Finally, the theme is highlighted through Dickens's choice of vocabulary with its repeated references to the file, leg-irons, chains and other means of restraint. Look at the annotated examples below.

Key quotations

... think for a moment of the long chain of iron or gold, of thorns or flowers, that would never have bound you, but for the formation of the first link on one memorable day. *(Volume 1, Chapter 9)*

Dickens invites his readers to consider their own lives and creates an interesting effect by suggesting that 'chains' that bind us can be made of very different materials – iron, gold, thorns or flowers – but that irrespective of what they are made of, they still enclose us and limit our freedom.

... the wretched man, after loading wretched me with his gold and silver chains for years, had risked his life to come to me, and I held it there in my keeping! *(Volume 2, Chapter 39)*

Dickens creates an unusual effect here by making Pip complain about being loaded with riches. He creates a contrast between the repeated word 'wretched', which suggests worthlessness, and the valuable 'gold and silver'. Another reference to 'chains' reminds us of Pip's obligations and responsibility to his benefactor.

What I was chained to, and how heavily, became intelligible to me, as I heard his hoarse voice, and sat looking up at his furrowed bald head... *(Volume 3, Chapter 40)*

Dickens repeatedly uses the idea that Pip is 'chained' to Magwitch and unable to free himself.

We see crimes committed and criminals punished in the novel and Dickens's language keeps the theme uppermost in the reader's mind. This theme is also linked to the themes of violence and justice.

Activity 6

a) Re-read Volume 2, Chapters 20, 28 and 32 and Volume 3, Chapter 56. Collect evidence to show whether or not you think Dickens approved of the way criminals were treated. Look carefully at the language he uses.

b) In small groups, write a page about Dickens's attitudes towards justice and punishment.

Love and loyalty

The themes of love and loyalty can be seen throughout the plot and between the characters. Dickens presents romantic love in Pip's adoration of Estella; he looks at love between 'parents' and their children, notably in the relationship between Pip and Joe; and he explores love and loyalty between comrades, as in Pip's relationship with Herbert and Magwitch's devoted patronage of Pip. It is evident that Dickens wants his readers to consider the importance of love and loyalty in shaping character and in bringing happiness or misery. He also highlights the themes of love and loyalty by contrasting them with significant acts of hatred and betrayal that occur in the novel.

Great Expectations is partly a love story and, although we may find it difficult to see much romance in the novel, due to Estella's complete indifference to Pip for almost the entire book, Pip's pursuit of her is a critical strand of the plot and a major theme. Pip's devotion to Estella, despite her cold treatment of him, shows his capacity for great loyalty; ultimately his loyalty pays off and the final chapter suggests a reunion.

Other love stories are presented slightly more conventionally. Herbert has a strong attachment to Clara Barley, whose very brief appearance shows her to be a sweet, kind girl and an ideal match for Herbert.

Dickens's rewriting of the ending of *Great Expectations* suggests that Pip and Estella might ultimately be united

Biddy outgrows her obvious romantic interest in Pip. She forgives him for his snobbish treatment of her and finds real happiness with a respectable man of her own class, whose kind and gentle nature she truly values. She still has a sisterly affection for Pip, however, and shows concern about his future and his broken "poor dream" *(Volume 3, Chapter 59)*.

Wemmick is not a very romantic lover of Miss Skiffins and, although his wedding day is described most charmingly, his admission to Pip that his new wife is "such a manager of fowls, you have no idea" *(Volume 3, Chapter 55)* is typical of Wemmick's **pragmatic** attitude to life. Wemmick is also presented as a loyal friend to Pip.

> **pragmatic** very matter of fact

It is also worth considering how Miss Havisham views love. She sees herself as a victim, practically boasts to Pip of her "Broken!" *(Volume 1, Chapter 8)* heart and dedicates her life to creating a 'curse' *(Volume 1, Chapter 11)* on the man who jilted her. She devotes all her energies into fashioning Estella into a weapon to use against men. She uses Pip as an experiment to test Estella's capacity to ensnare and hurt the opposite sex and, in doing so, she destroys Pip's happiness by encouraging him to love Estella.

Key quotations

"Love her, love her, love her! If she favours you, love her. If she wounds you, love her. If she tears your heart to pieces—and as it gets older and stronger, it will tear deeper—love her, love her, love her!" *(Volume 2, Chapter 29)*

Dickens looks specifically at loyalty as an aspect of love. He does this through his presentation of several characters, one of whom is Joe. Joe is loyal to Pip throughout. He protects him as a child, remains a constant friend through his apprenticeship, is pleased for his good fortune and appears to bear no grudge against him. He nurses Pip back to health after his collapse, pays his debts for him and discreetly returns to the forge when he feels his job is done.

Another character loyal to Pip is Magwitch, whose brief encounter with a little boy who showed him kindness has changed him and come to dominate his life.

Key quotations

"Yes, Pip, dear boy, I've made a gentleman on you! It's me wot has done it! I swore that time, sure as ever I earned a guinea, that guinea should go to you. I swore arterwards, sure as ever I spec'lated and got rich, you should get rich. I lived rough, that you should live smooth; I worked hard, that you should be above work." *(Volume 2, Chapter 39)*

Despite Pip's initial revulsion at Magwitch, he eventually returns his affection and is loyal to him to the end.

Dickens uses **juxtaposition** to highlight the themes of love and loyalty by including acts of hate and betrayal that contrast with them.

The most significant act of betrayal in the novel is Compeyson's denouncement of Magwitch to the authorities, leading to Magwitch's capture and death. Compeyson's initial betrayal of him occurred before the story begins when he let Magwitch bear the major responsibility for his counterfeiting activities.

We have noted the malevolence of Orlick already. His hatred for Pip is most clearly presented in Volume 3, Chapter 53 when he lures Pip to the limekiln with the intention of murdering him. His main act of betrayal is to savagely attack Mrs Joe during the half-day holiday that Joe gave him.

> **juxtaposition** two different ideas or things placed side by side to create a specific effect

Activity 7

In pairs, find evidence to show Orlick's reasons for hating Pip so much.

Education and self-improvement

Education is a theme very clearly associated with Pip's development as we see him progress from a barely literate child to a man capable of reading foreign language texts aloud to Magwitch, who can't understand them.

Although Dickens shows the value of education, he also demonstrates through references to Compeyson, that the ability to read and write does not equate to 'goodness'.

At the beginning of the novel, Joe is unable to read anything beyond the letters that make up his name, but he is presented as the most admirable character in the novel. Pip tries, unsuccessfully to teach him to read. Biddy is more successful and possibly more patient in her teaching and we see in Chapter 57 in Volume 3 that Joe is able to write Pip a brief but dignified note.

There is more on education in the 'Context' section of this book.

Christian virtues

The Christian virtues of patience, diligence and forgiveness make up another lesser theme, which is also dealt with in the 'Context' section.

Writing about themes

Upgrade

In your assessment you may be asked to write about an individual theme or a pair of themes. There are different ways that such questions might be asked.

The first type of question is about how Dickens presents a theme, for example:

How does Dickens present the theme of identity in *Great Expectations*?

This type of question requires that you think about the methods the novelist has used to convey this theme. To answer, you will need to consider the writer's methods of presentation, for example through:

- the novel's title
- the plot
- whether characters discuss the theme
- whether characters, through their actions, 'do' (or don't do) the theme
- whether the theme is reinforced through reference to linked ideas/themes or in figurative language
- whether the theme is presented as a contrast or opposite to another theme.

The second type of question asks you to consider the relative importance of the theme, for example:

How important do you think the theme of guilt and remorse is in the novel?

How far do you consider the novel to be about social class?

To answer this type of question, you may find it useful to ask yourself how many of the bullet points above apply to the theme in the question. You might also consider how the theme relates to:

- other significant themes
- Dickens's purpose/message.

The third type of question that may focus on theme is an extract-based question, for example:

Read the following passage from Volume 1, Chapter 7 and then answer the question that follows. In this extract Joe tells Pip about his childhood and his parents. The extract is from: '"Why didn't you ever go to school, Joe, when you were as little as me?"' to 'Whatsume'er the failings on his part, Remember reader he were that good in his heart.'

Starting with this extract, write about how Dickens presents the theme of parenting in the novel.

You should write about:

a) how Dickens presents the theme in this extract
b) how Dickens presents the theme of parenting elsewhere in the novel.

Remember that you will never be asked in an exam about a theme that is not very important. However, the theme might be expressed slightly differently from what you are expecting, so make sure that you think carefully before beginning your answer.

Preparing for the exam

Make sure you are fully prepared for the challenges of the assessment by following this step-by-step revision programme.

Step 1: Make sure you know the novel really well

Great Expectations is quite a long novel, and Dickens's vocabulary is occasionally challenging, so you should try to read it at least three times before you go into the exam. You can also listen to an audio-book of the novel to keep it fresh in your mind.

As you re-read it, jot down some notes under the following headings:

- Plot and structure
- Characters
- Themes
- Context
- Language.

Just before the exam, re-read the chapter on plot and structure in this book.

Step 2: Revision

Go back through this book and check that you have done all of the activities either in class, in pairs or groups, or on your own.

Re-read all the 'Upgrade' sections in this book, where you will find tips for tackling questions and improving your answers.

Re-read all the key quotes from *Great Expectations* in this book. Try to memorize as many as you can. Your assessment may be partly based on an extract from the novel but you will always be tested on your knowledge of the book as a whole. You will need to support your answers with quotations, so it is vital that you are well prepared.

Tips for assessment

Make sure you have learned some key quotations that relate to:

- each major character
- some of the minor characters
- key themes.

You should also be able to quote examples that show you understand some of Dickens's techniques with language.

Revision exercises – extract-based questions

Activity 1

Prepare for an 'extract'-based question by opening the novel randomly, choose any 'half page' and write at least one paragraph about the extract in relation to:

- plot and structure
- context
- characters
- language
- themes.

The extract from Volume 1, Chapter 1 below shows how a student has annotated an extract, looking for significant elements, in order to complete this revision exercise.

The repetition of the phrase 'I would' creates a 'child-like' style

I said that I would get him the file, and I would get him what broken bits of food I could, and I would come to him at the Battery, early in the morning.

Magwitch forcing Pip to swear an oath links to

"Say Lord strike you dead if you don't!" said the man.

I said so, and he took me down.

Christian context

"Now," he pursued, "you remember what you've undertook, and you remember that young man, and you get home!"

Pip calls Magwitch 'Sir': for respect/ innocence

Pip's fear: shown through his stuttering 'goo-good' as well as the description 'faltered'

"Goo-good night, sir," I faltered.

Magwitch's joke about being a 'frog or a eel' shows a lighter side of his character

"Much of that!" said he, glancing about him over the cold wet flat. "I wish I was a frog. Or a eel!"

Through Pip's sympathetic eyes we see Magwitch's suffering –'shuddering body', 'limped'

At the same time, he hugged his shuddering body in both his arms, clasping himself, as if to hold himself together—and limped towards the low church wall. As I saw him go, picking his way among the nettles, and among the brambles that bound the green mounds, he looked in my young eyes as if he were eluding the hands of the dead people, stretching up cautiously out of their graves, to get a twist upon his ankle and pull him in.

'bound' is a motif of emprisonment

Dickens reminds us, this is the perspective of little Pip

When he came to the low church wall, he got over it, like a man whose legs were numbed and stiff, and then turned round to look for me. When I saw him turning, I set my face towards home, and made the best use of my legs. But presently I looked over my shoulder, and saw him going on again towards the river, still hugging himself in both arms, and picking his way with his sore feet among the great stones dropped into the marshes here and there, for stepping-places when the rains were heavy or the tide was in,

Suggesting Pip's bond with Magwitch

The description of the marshes, river and the sky makes the landscape seem dreary and never-ending

The marshes were just a long black horizontal line then, as I stopped to look after him; and the river was just another horizontal line, not nearly so broad nor yet so black; and the sky was just a row of long angry red lines and dense black lines intermixed. On the edge of the river I could faintly make out the only two black things in all the prospect that seemed to be standing upright; one of these was the beacon by which the sailors steered—like an unhooped cask upon a pole—an ugly thing when you were near it; the other, a gibbet, with some chains hanging to it which had once held a pirate. The man was limping on towards this latter, as if he were the pirate come to life, and come down, and going back to hook himself up again. It gave me a terrible turn when I thought so; and as I saw the cattle lifting their heads to gaze after him, I wondered whether they thought so too . I looked all round for the horrible young man, and could see no signs of him. But now I was frightened again, and ran home without stopping.

A gruesome image; linking to crime and punishment

Foreshadows Magwitch's fate: returning to the gibbet and certain death

Pip's vivid imagination is shown here

The young Pip runs home not to safety but to a violent sister

And these are the candidate's paragraphs.

Plot & Structure

This extract from the opening of the novel begins the exposition of the story; presenting the key event of Pip's young life – his encounter with Magwitch. Pip's promise to help Magwitch creates feelings of gratitude in the convict which lead directly to Pip's 'great expectations'.

Context

It is Christmas Eve when Pip was about seven years old; the setting for the meeting is the isolated churchyard. Dickens has set the novel early in the nineteenth century as the Hulks were not used after 1843. Magwitch's insistence that Pip swears an oath, to return, places the action in a Christian context.

Characters

Dickens presents Pip as a polite, respectful boy, who calls Magwitch 'sir' despite his wretched appearance. Pip's innocence is shown as he believes in the 'terrible young man'. Pip is sympathetic to Magwitch, describing his 'sore feet'. Pip's vivid imagination is shown as he imagines Magwitch re-hooking himself into the gibbet.

Magwitch is presented as a wretched man, desperate for help. Although he threatens Pip he also jokes with him and seems concerned that he gets home. Hugging himself as if 'to hold himself together' (p.5) Magwitch is presented sympathetically.

Language

There are three 'voices' in this extract; the child-like voice of Pip who uses simple sentence construction and repetition; the uneducated speech of the older, coarser Magwitch, "Say Lord strike you dead if you don't!" where the exclamation mark at the end of the oath suggests his intimidating nature. We also hear the more cultured voice of the older Pip, looking back at 'little Pip' with some amusement. The use of the complex words 'eluding' rather than 'dodging' and 'cautiously' rather than 'carefully' reflect a more educated voice.

There are some motifs evident in this extract that recur throughout the novel, including reference to chains and other restraints like the nettles that 'bound' the graves, for example; by introducing these ideas so early, Dickens alerts the reader to their significance later on. Dickens uses colour to present the dismal landscape; the 'green mounds' are graves; the marshes are 'black' and gloomy; the sky is described, ominously, as 'red' and 'black' intermixed.

Themes

The theme of crime, punishment and justice is immediately presented in Magwitch's situation as an escapee. The description of the grisly gibbet and the hanged pirate reinforce this.

This early memory of Pip's shows him on his first step of a journey that will explore his growing up and his search for identity in this Bildungsroman novel.

Essay-style questions

Activity 2

1. Prepare for essay-style questions by choosing one of the following themes from the novel and writing a page or more about its importance:

   - identity
   - children and parents
   - crime, punishment and justice
   - what it is to be a gentleman
   - love and loyalty.

2. Choose any character from the novel and practise writing a page or more about how Dickens presents the character. Write a further page about the function of the character in the novel. Find relevant quotations from the novel to support your ideas.

Step 3: Before the exam

There are two broad categories of questions at this level:

- extract-based questions, which include a printed extract of between approximately 300 and 500 words. These are frequently divided into two parts. Part (a) is focused on analysis of some aspect of the extract, while Part (b) is focused on the wider novel

- essay-style questions, which demand reference to aspects found in the novel as a whole.

Extract-based questions

a) Explore how Dickens presents Pip's thoughts and feelings about Biddy in this extract.
Give examples from the extract to support your ideas.

"You are one of those, Biddy," said I, "who make the most of every chance. You never had a chance before you came here, and see how improved you are!" […]

"Well!" said I, "we must talk together a little more, as we used to do. And I must consult you a little more, as I used to do. Let us have a quiet walk on the marshes next Sunday, Biddy, and a long chat."

b) Explain how Pip's relationship with Biddy is presented elsewhere in the novel.

In your answer you should consider:

- Biddy's attitude towards Pip
- Pip's attempt to make amends with Biddy.

For extract-based questions you should look at past paper questions and specimen questions to see the precise format of question used in the exam you are going to take.

You will have to practise reading the printed extract really carefully and working closely on Dickens's use of language.

Although the starting point will be the extract, there will be a specific focus to the question, so you will not simply be expected to write about its significant features as we did in Activity 1.

Whatever the focus of the question, it is a good strategy to begin your answer by briefly identifying:

- the context of the extract
- its significance in the novel as a whole
- the main mood, atmosphere or tone of the extract.

Before you start writing about the extract:

- Read the question(s) that are set on the extract very carefully and make sure you understand what you are being asked to do.
- Read the extract at least twice with the questions in mind, the first time to remind yourself of the content and context of the extract.
- The second time you read it through, highlight and/or annotate it, making sure that you focus on aspects of Dickens's presentation of material (for example, characters or theme) and paying particular attention to the focus of the question.
- Work methodically from the start to finish of the extract.
- Never just list language features such as alliteration, use of simile or personification without explaining the effects Dickens intends/achieves.

Essay-style questions

Most essay-style questions will ask you to write about plot (the events that take place in the novel), structure (the way the novel is organized and develops), characters (and their relationships) or themes. However, these questions will never simply require a description of these elements. You will always be expected to consider the ways in which these aspects are presented or their significance in the novel.

Here are some typical essay-style questions, followed by an explanation of what each question requires and an outline plan for tackling the question:

How does Dickens present the character of Jaggers in the novel?

This question is about character and the 'how' part of the question refers to Dickens's methods. His methods for creating character include:

- what the character looks/sounds like
- what the character says about himself/herself and about others

- what others say about the character
- contrast/comparison with other characters
- what the character does – his/her actions and/or reactions in the novel
- what kind of language the character uses when speaking.

How is the theme of identity presented in 'Great Expectations'?

This question is about theme and the 'how' part of the question refers to the methods that Dickens used to present the theme, for example:

- through the content of the novel, its plot
- through characters discussing the theme
- through the actions of characters that may be said to 'do' the theme
- through repeated motifs and/or in figurative language
- through the presentation of 'paired' themes or 'opposites'
- through characters acting as a 'mouthpiece' for Dickens's views on the theme.

Use the bulleted list as headings for your plan and make sure you refer to each relevant aspect in your answer.

***Great Expectations* is sometimes described as 'a novel about criminality'. Do you agree with this description?**

This question is about the nature of the novel as a whole. The command words, 'Do you agree?' mean that you should weigh up the evidence for agreeing with the description. A good way to tackle questions like this is to consider the appropriateness of the statement in relation to plot, characters, themes, structure and mood/atmosphere.

Activity 3

1. Create a plan for each of the example questions above. Try to organize each plan so that related points are grouped together.
2. Find quotations to support your proposed argument.

Step 4: Answering the question

Always make a plan before you start writing an essay-based answer. The plan will help you to:

- structure your answer logically
- target the precise demands of the question
- avoid missing out points that are crucial to your argument
- include appropriate quotations.

Don't spend more than about five minutes or so on a plan. Use the first few minutes as thinking time, then jot down your ideas and away you go!

Always write a brief introduction that is targeted directly on the question.

Develop your answer, step by step, building your argument by referring to precise moments in the novel.

Always support your ideas with short, apt quotations from the novel. The best way to use quotation is to 'absorb' it into your own sentences. For example:

> Joe is also shown to be very modest and dutiful, explaining how he worked "tolerable hard" to keep the "pot a biling" and to provide for his parents rather than relying on them for his upkeep. This is one of the reasons why Joe didn't go to school as he was effectively the only bread-winner in the family. This example creates an impression of Joe as a selfless young man, willing to take on the responsibilities that his father should have shouldered.

The candidate makes the point that Joe was modest and dutiful and then illustrates that with a quotation, which provides evidence of his modesty and sense of duty. Finally the student explains how this contributes to Dickens's characterization of Joe.

Keep a close eye on the time in the exam. Make sure you know in advance how much time you can spend on each part of the paper and stick to it! Try to avoid leaving an answer unfinished. It is always better to end your answer with a short, neat conclusion rather than stopping abruptly or dashing down final thoughts in note form.

Sample questions

1

How does Dickens present the changing relationship between Pip and Estella as they grow from children to adults?

2

Explore how Dickens presents ideas about what makes a good parent through the presentation of Miss Havisham, in this extract and elsewhere in the novel.
In this extract Miss Havisham accuses Estella of being cold and unfeeling towards her.
The extract is from 'We were seated by the fire, as just now described, and Miss Havisham still had Estella's arm drawn through her own, and still clutched Estella's hand in hers, when Estella gradually began to detach herself.' to '"Did I never give her love!" cried Miss Havisham, turning wildly to me.' *(Volume 2, Chapter 38)*

3

How far do you agree with the view that it is hard to retain the reader's sympathy for Pip, through what has been described as a 'snob's progress'?

4

How does Dickens explore the theme of 'crime and punishment' in *Great Expectations*?

5

Choose any **two** of the characters listed below and explain what they contribute to the novel as a whole.
Pumblechook, Wopsle, the Aged P, Biddy, Orlick

6

Dickens is much admired for the comedy of his writing. Choose at least two sections from the novel that you find especially comical and explain what methods Dickens has used to amuse you.

7

Read the extract below and then answer the following questions:
a) How does Dickens present Magwitch in the extract below?
b) How does Dickens present Magwitch after his return from New South Wales?
Extract from
'"Hold your noise!" cried a terrible voice, as a man started up from among the graves at the side of the church porch. "Keep still, you little devil, or I'll cut your throat!"'
to
'"Blacksmith, eh?" said he. And looked down at his leg.' *(Volume 1, Chapter 1)*

Sample answers
Sample answer 1

Explore how Dickens presents the relationship between Pip and Magwitch in this extract and elsewhere in the novel.

In this extract, Pip has brought food and a file to Magwitch and watches him eat.

The extract is from '"What's in the bottle, boy?" said he.' to 'I had often watched a large dog of ours eating his food; and I now noticed a decided similarity between the dog's way of eating, and the man's.' *(Volume 1, Chapter 3)*

A clear start.

Good focus on the terms of the question.

Consistent attention on the relationship here – good.

Quite a sensitive reading of Pip's changing relationship to the man who frightened him.

This extract is taken from Volume 1, Chapter 3 of the novel and we see Pip has brought food to Magwitch who greedily devours it. The setting is the cold and misty marshland, and Dickens's intentions are to show the beginning of the relationship between Pip and Magwitch. At this stage there is not much of a relationship between them. Pip is afraid of Magwitch when he first meets him, but here he seems to pity him and his suffering. Dickens presents Magwitch as being in a desperate state of cold and hunger: 'He shivered all the while' and he creates some humour by telling us that his shivering was so violent that he nearly bit the top off the brandy bottle. The fact that Pip is able to use this light tone suggests that he was no longer as afraid of Magwitch as before. The relationship of bully and victim has changed as Pip sees Magwitch as a poor victim himself.

Pip shows concern for Magwitch as a fellow creature, sympathizing with him about his ague. Pip sounds more grown-up here, almost as if he is copying what he has heard grown-ups say about the marshes, "they're dreadful aguish. Rheumatic, too." This suggests a more patronizing relationship between them, with Pip pitying Magwitch. This patronizing relationship is also seen in the way that Pip watches Magwitch 'gobbling' his food and he compares him to his dog at home. The fact that he can look at Magwitch and see him as a dumb animal chomping at his food suggests that he is patronizing him. It also suggests that he is less afraid of him because he reminds him of his pet.

Pip has shown himself to be trustworthy and as good as his promise. Magwitch is grateful to Pip for the food and the brandy. Hearing a noise, Magwitch has a moment of doubt about Pip, saying suddenly, "You're not a deceiving imp? You brought no one with you?", but when he is reassured he relaxes a little and admits, "I believe you", showing that the relationship of trust developing between them.

Quotation is used well to support ideas.

Magwitch is moved by Pip's charity and that is when his voice clicks 'like a clock' and he wipes tears from his eyes 'with his ragged rough sleeve'. Dickens shows that Magwitch is capable of feelings through this mannerism and we are prepared for the relationship to develop later in the novel. When Pip says that he is glad that Magwitch is enjoying the food, Magwitch replies, "Thankee, my boy". This is the first sign of a father-son relationship, which Magwitch is keen to rekindle when he returns from Australia at the end of Volume 2, announcing, "Look'ee here, Pip. I'm your second father. You're my son—more to me nor any son."

Retains focus on Dickens's methods.

This is a good example of a smooth transition from the extract to the wider novel.

When Magwitch turns up so unexpectedly at Pip's door and claims him as his son, he gets a very cool reception from 23-year-old Pip. While Magwitch has spent the years apart dreaming of making Pip a gentleman, Pip has done his best to forget about his convict and even comforted himself with the thought that he was at least a very long way off and 'might be veritably dead'. The relationship is very uneven here as Magwitch is full of affection for the boy who 'kep life' in him, while Pip is revolted by his appearance, his coarse manners and his presumption in kissing Pip's hands, while Pip's 'blood ran cold' at the convict's touch.

A good paragraph; well-focused on the relationship and with good support.

Magwitch's return dashes all Pip's dreams about Estella and his future, and he finds it difficult to conceal his disgust at his benefactor's affection. It is Herbert who persuades Pip that he must help Magwitch evade the authorities and the death penalty he would face if arrested as a returned 'lifer'. Once Pip has heard Magwitch's miserable life story and learned about the injustice that he has suffered, he sees a softer man beneath the surface and feels a duty towards the man who has risked everything to see his 'gentleman'. The bond that was made in the lonely churchyard now becomes one that is not broken until Magwitch's death with Pip by his side.

A nice link is made between the two different parts of the novel.

This is good work with an appropriate focus for most of the time. Occasionally, it loses focus; for example, the point about Pip copying grown-up comments is a fair one but not strictly relevant to the relationship between Magwitch and Pip. The candidate quotes from the extract and from the wider novel in a purposeful way.

Sample answer 2

> How important is the character of Orlick in *Great Expectations*? With reference to at least two different sections, discuss Orlick's function in the novel.

A focused start.

Orlick is a key character in 'Great Expectations'. He is the moody journeyman that Joe employs at the forge. Dickens puts Orlick in the novel to be jealous of Pip and to be his enemy.

Useful quotation and evident knowledge/ understanding.

When Orlick is first introduced in the novel, Dickens describes him fairly negatively: 'He was a broadshouldered loose-limbed swarthy fellow of great strength, never in a hurry, and always slouching.' Additionally, he is described as 'resentful' and Pip recalls that when he was little, Orlick tried to scare him with talk of the Devil, who he claimed lived at the back of the forge. Orlick's jealousy of Pip helps to further the plot and gives him a reason to try to halt Pip's plot to get Magwitch out of the country.

Although this paragraph reveals knowledge of Orlick's character, it is less focused on his function.

Like Pip, Orlick works in the forge and is subject to the wrath of Mrs Joe. We only actually witness Mrs Joe abusing Orlick once, earlier on the day that she is attacked and left for dead. She calls him a 'great idle hulker' and causes a fight between Orlick and Joe, which Joe easily wins. However, Orlick suggests, in his taunting of Pip at the limekiln, that he was more regularly bullied, stating that Pip 'was favoured' and that he, Orlick, 'was bullied and beat'. He gives this as his reason for trying to kill Mrs Joe.

This is more clearly linked to function and the candidate makes an interesting point.

In this way, we find that Orlick acts partly as a foil for Pip, who must endure his sister's abuse without striking back at her. It is possible to see, in Orlick's attack on Mrs Joe, some kind of wish-fulfilment of Pip's, although Dickens does not make this explicit in his presentation of the character or the crime.

The focus is more on Pip than Orlick, but the point about the love triangle suggests understanding of Orlick's function without being explicit.

Another similarity between Orlick and Pip relates to Biddy, who Orlick admires. Biddy is wary of Orlick and tells Pip that she doesn't like the way he 'dances at' her. Pip is affronted by Orlick's interest in Biddy even though he shows very little romantic interest in her himself. But there is a clear hint that Pip's determination to block Orlick's attentions to Biddy arises from a form of jealousy that Pip cannot quite admit to. He admits to the reader that he wanted to have Orlick 'dismissed' however and that is a wish not entirely unconnected with his recognition that Biddy is 'immeasurably better than Estella' and that therefore he and Orlick are in some kind of 'romantic triangle' with Biddy.

Pip may not have Orlick dismissed from his place at the forge, as he wished to do, because of Mrs Joe's 'sudden fancy for him', but he does succeed in getting him dismissed from Miss Havisham's employment by mentioning to Jaggers that he 'doubted Orlick's being the right sort of man to fill a post of trust at Miss Havisham's'. This gives Orlick further motivation to try to kill Pip and he functions as a great source of tension in Chapter 53 of Volume 3 as he goads Pip about all his grudges against him. Orlick flees when the rescue party arrive.

Orlick's function in creating tension is well conveyed here.

Dickens's novel is highly patterned as Orlick is Pip's arch-enemy in the same way that Compeyson acts as Magwitch's arch-enemy. Both men are entirely malicious and self-serving, and one of Orlick's functions in the novel is to echo Compeyson's criminal tendencies, although in a much cruder and more violent form.

A clear link is made between Orlick and Compeyson.

Dickens compares Orlick to two notoriously 'bad' characters from the Bible: Cain, who murdered his brother Abel in the book of Genesis in the Old Testament, and also the 'wandering Jew', a figure from the New Testament, who was said to have mocked Christ on his way to the cross. This fairly emphatically marks out his function in the novel to be a force for the bad.

Another good paragraph, this reveals a secure understanding of Dickens's craft as a writer.

This is a clearly written and well-supported exploration of Orlick's function. The candidate reveals a secure understanding of the importance of the character. Sometimes the focus of the answer wavers from Orlick, but the candidate succeeds in conveying the impression of close engagement with the text.

Glossary

ague a fever, much like the 'flu

allegory a piece of literature which carries a spiritual, moral or political meaning and in which characters and/or events are clearly symbolic of something else

aristocracy people whose ancestors received from a king or queen land and/or titles that have been passed down through the generations. The titles have their own fine distinctions

aside a remark by a character in a play, made directly to the audience, which the other characters supposedly do not hear

asseverate to insist seriously

avaricious greedy for money or personal gain

baronet an aristocrat ranked below a baron but above a knight, addressed as 'Sir' like a knight

benefactor a supporter with good intentions; in this novel, the word implies financial support

Bildungsroman a novel about the early years of somebody's life, exploring the development of his or her character and personality

caricature an exaggerated and often comical presentation of a character; presented in words or as a cartoon

chronological order the order in which events happened, from the earliest to the latest

coat of arms a unique design of symbols and colours, drawn/painted on a shield to represent an individual or family; coats of arms originated in medieval times

conciliatory aimed at keeping the peace

corn-chandler a trader who sells corn

dialect a regional variety of language, in which words are pronounced differently in different parts of the country or unique words are used

diffidence a shy, hesitant approach to life

discrimination the ability to make accurate judgements

figurative language any language, including metaphors and similes, that is used in a non-literal way

first person the use of the pronouns 'I' and 'me'. In a story written in the first person the narrator is usually telling a story in which he or she has a major role. Such a perspective allows intimate access to the narrator's thoughts but no access into the inner workings of the other characters

foil a contrast to something else

foreshadowing (or proleptic irony) when a character says or experiences something that becomes significant later in the novel

genre a literary category such as comedy, tragedy, romance

genteel well-mannered and refined

gibbet a scaffold built for the purpose of hanging criminals

hard labour the back-breaking work many prisoners were sentenced to carry out, such as breaking rocks in a quarry, building roads or labouring on the docks. Some prisoners had to walk a treadmill all day with no end product but exhaustion

hierarchy a system of ranking, from the most superior to the most inferior

Hulks old warships moored in rivers and harbours served as temporary prisons at the time the novel was set, used when regular prisons were full to capacity

idiosyncrasy a recognizable personal habit

impetuosity a tendency to act impulsively

implausible far-fetched; creative yet improbable; for example, wearing the same dress for 20 years without it falling in rags

indentures the contract made between an apprentice and his employer

Industrial Revolution a time when more people began to work in industry rather than agriculture. They left the countryside and moved close to the factories and mills in large cities, from where the manufactured goods were exported

ingratiate oneself to seek approval of another person, usually in an attempt to gain some benefit

innate natural; present from birth

jilted abandoned, usually on a wedding day

journeyman a fully trained worker in a craft or trade, employed/paid by the day

journeyman a fully trained worker in a craft or trade, employed/paid by the day

juxtaposition two different ideas or things placed side by side to create a specific effect

Lifer a criminal transported to Australia for life

limekiln a place where quicklime, a chemical associated with the disposal of dead bodies, is made

malevolent having bad intentions

mangy suggests both messy and dirty

mercenary motivated by money

metaphor a word or phrase that compares one thing with another without using 'like' or 'as', e.g. 'As I watched them… enjoying themselves so much, I thought what terrible good sauce for a dinner my fugitive friend on the marshes was…'

motif a word, phrase or image repeated to create specific effects, e.g. hands in *Great Expectations*

nemesis an arch-enemy

obsequious grovelling; excessively flattering

omniscient knowing everything, as an omniscient narrator does about the characters, including their inner thoughts and motivations

penitent showing or feeling sorrow for wrong-doing

perspective in literature, point of view; perception of the situation

pilgrimage a journey made to a 'sacred' or 'holy' place with the intention of becoming a better person; here the word is a metaphor for Pip's journey and moral progress

plot device a character or an incident in a novel or play whose function is to make the plot work or to make themes more prominent to the reader

pragmatic very matter of fact

redemption and salvation terms that refer to the belief in Christian teaching that people can be forgiven for their sins and live with God forever in heaven

repressed desires feelings that people have but try to deny or hide from themselves

simile figure of speech that compares one thing with another using 'like' or 'as' to highlight the similarity, e.g. 'she pounced on me like an eagle on a lamb'

social mobility the ability of members of the lower classes to acquire wealth through their own efforts and 'rise' up the class system, rather than being born into a moneyed background

spendthrift someone who spends money freely and without regard to cost

symbol a word or object used to represent a different word or object, e.g. Dickens frequently uses 'chain' to suggest oppressive duties

syndetic the use of conjunctions (e.g. 'and' or 'but') joining different parts of a sentence together

toady a false flatterer

tumble up suggests a childhood with little guidance and many accidents

tripling a device where a writer groups statements, verbs, nouns or adjectives into sequences of three to create an emphatic or comical effect, e.g. 'But there was a calm, a rest, a virtuous hush'

varmint (Magwitch pronounces it 'warmint') the local dialect version of 'vermin', the name given to troublesome small animals or insects such as rats and cockroaches

OXFORD
UNIVERSITY PRESS

Great Clarendon Street, Oxford OX2 6DP United Kingdom

Oxford University Press is a department of the University of Oxford. It furthers the University's objective of excellence in research, scholarship, and education by publishing worldwide. Oxford is a registered trade mark of Oxford University Press in the UK and in certain other countries

British Library Cataloguing in Publication Data

Data available

ISBN 978-0-19-835528-1

10 9 8 7 6 5 4 3 2 1

Printed in Great Britain by Ashford Print and Publishing Services, Gosport

Acknowledgements

Cover: Doug Armand/Getty Images; **p1:** Doug Armand/Getty Images; **p6:** Copyright Supplied by Capital Pictures; **p11:** © Robbie Jack/Robbie Jack/Corbis; **p15:** ITV/REX; **p20:** © The Art Archive/Alamy; **p25:** © AF archive/Alamy; **p29:** Moviestore/REX; **p36:** © Steve Vidler/Alamy; **p37:** © Lebrecht Authors/Lebrecht Music & Arts/Lebrecht Music & Arts/Corbis; **p39:** Hulton Archive/Getty Images; **p41:** © Mary Evans Picture Library/Alamy; **p45:** © The Art Archive/Alamy; **p46:** Copyright Supplied by Capital Pictures; **p51:** © AF archive/Alamy; **p54:** Moviestore/REX; **p57:** Alastair Muir/REX; **p62:** REX; **p64:** Copyright Supplied by Capital Pictures; **p72:** © Moviestore collection Ltd/Alamy; **p76:** © Sophie Davies/Alamy; **p81:** © The Art Archive/Alamy; **p85:** REX; **p89:** © Pictorial Press Ltd/Alamy; **p91:** © WENN UK/Alamy; **p94:** © Pictorial Press Ltd/Alamy

Extracts are taken from the Rollercoasters edition of Charles Dickens: *Great Expectations* (Oxford University Press, 2015).